MW01120596

Framing Sexual and Domestic Violence through Language

List of Previous Publications

Klein, R. (2012). *Responding to Intimate Violence against Women: The Role of Informal Networks.*

Klein, R. C. A., and B. Wallner, eds. (2004). *Conflict, Gender, and Violence.*

Klein, R. C. A., ed. (1998). *Multidisciplinary Perspectives on Family Violence.*

Framing Sexual and Domestic Violence through Language

Edited by Renate Klein

palgrave
macmillan

HUMBER LIBRARIES LAKESHORE CAMPUS
3199 Lakeshore Blvd West
TORONTO, ON. M8V 1K8

FRAMING SEXUAL AND DOMESTIC VIOLENCE THROUGH LANGUAGE
Copyright © Renate Klein, 2013.

All rights reserved.

First published in 2013 by PALGRAVE MACMILLAN® in the United States—a division of St. Martin's Press LLC, 175 Fifth Avenue, New York, NY 10010.

Where this book is distributed in the UK, Europe and the rest of the world, this is by Palgrave Macmillan, a division of Macmillan Publishers Limited, registered in England, company number 785998, of Houndmills, Basingstoke, Hampshire RG21 6XS.

Palgrave Macmillan is the global academic imprint of the above companies and has companies and representatives throughout the world.

Palgrave® and Macmillan® are registered trademarks in the United States, the United Kingdom, Europe and other countries.

ISBN: 978-1-137-34008-5

Library of Congress Cataloging-in-Publication Data

Framing sexual and domestic violence through language / edited by Renate Klein.
    pages cm
Includes bibliographical references and index.
ISBN 978-1-137-34008-5 (alk. paper)
    1. Family violence. 2. Sex crimes. 3. Sexual abuse victims. 4. Sexism in language. 5. Sexism in communication. 6. Language and sex. 7. Sociolinguistics. I. Klein, Renate, 1959–

HV6626.F698 2013
362.82'92014—dc23 2013011854

A catalogue record of the book is available from the British Library.

Design by Scribe Inc.

First edition: September 2013

10 9 8 7 6 5 4 3 2 1

HUMBER LIBRARIES LAKESHORE CAMPUS
3199 Lakeshore Blvd West
TORONTO, ON, M8V 1K8

Contents

Illustrations

Just Words?

Purpose, Translation, and Metaphor in Framing Sexual and Domestic Violence through Language

Renate Klein, United States/United Kingdom

This book examines how sexual and domestic violence against women is framed through language. The contributors are concerned with the expressions used to name abuse, the meanings suggested by these expressions, and their implications for research, policy, and practice. Language use, for better or worse, shapes the process of perceiving, interpreting, and responding to abuse. From the phrasing of survey questions to news coverage, police reports, policy directives, and everyday day talk, how things are said is not a matter of "just words" but of the right words.

Although language use has been discussed extensively in terms of what somebody means by expressions like *violence against women, domestic violence,* or *honor killing*, little terminology is widely agreed (Wilcox 2006). Harmful practices against women also occur outside of intimate or family relationships, but for abuses within these contexts alone a plethora of English terms are in use, such as *domestic violence/abuse, sexual violence/abuse, sexualized violence, violence against women, wife abuse, dating violence, battering, sexual assault, intimate partner violence/abuse, honor-based violence, gender-based violence,* and *gender or gendered violence*. As these terms differ in focus, scope, conceptual ancestry, and policy implications, their appropriateness for different purposes is contested (see also Wright and Hearn in this volume). The struggle for properly naming "it" (the nature and quality of harmful practices) continues, and the link between "it" and its many names remains tenuous. One might think that over the course of the past forty years terminology has been agreed and disputes over how to speak about "it" are a thing of the past. This is not so. If anything—as the range, diversity, and complexity of harmful practices against women has become clearer—terminology is increasingly fragmented and language use as challenging as ever.

This challenge may be less obvious where speakers share a common professional background and language. Within certain limits terminology may indeed be agreed and language use unproblematic. However, when looking across niches of shared language use, the multiplicity of names and thus the ambiguity of meanings become more obvious. This, at least, has been the experience of the contributors to this book. They come from different countries and work in different languages, disciplines, and intellectual traditions. This also means that they draw on different empirical evidence and theoretical concepts. It is from this vantage point that the book explores language use within and across cultural contexts. The contributors are not putting themselves forward as experts in linguistics or discourse analysis but as researchers who grapple with language issues in their daily work.

The book is based on an experiment in collaborative working, in which space was deliberately made to register misunderstandings as they arose in the process of discussion and that in turn helped to explore the significant subtleties of language use. Through this dedicated attention to language and languages, three broad themes emerged that form the conceptual background to this book: the purpose of language (language for knowledge, for public awareness, and for institutional change), the significance of translation, and the role of metaphor.

The Study Circle Process and Chapter Overview

The book emerged from a collaborative process among the contributing authors. Its topic and approach grew out of a dedicated process of close discussion that went beyond presenting papers. The contributors formed a study circle with the explicit goal of discussing their respective work through the lens of naming, word choice, and language use. The purpose of this was to dedicate attention to an issue that tends to be pushed to the sidelines of ordinary research activity. The study circle process has been the vehicle for uncovering misunderstandings that arise from naming across contexts. This approach made it possible to notice, and indeed welcome, misunderstandings and accord them proper space in the analytical process. As a collaborative process of discussion and reflection during two intensive workshops, one year apart, the study circle has been an experimental process for all contributors. The book as a whole does not offer better language but examines the challenges associated with language use across academic, cultural, and national contexts.

The contexts examined in this book include the wording of questions and the reporting of findings in French survey research (Condon, Chapter 3); case descriptions of domestic violence homicides in Swiss police reports (Gloor and Meier, Chapter 4); descriptions of domestic violence cases in Polish print magazines and private assertions about hypothetical scenarios of domestic violence (Kwiatkowska, Chapter 5); policy statements by British governmental and nongovernmental agencies and reflections about violence by men who are active in antiviolence work (Wright and Hearn, Chapter 2); public statements about the killings of women in the name of family honor in Denmark (Mogensen, Chapter 7); descriptions of intervention programs for perpetrators of domestic violence in Denmark (Sørensen, Chapter 6); and statements by middle managers at an educational institution in the United States (Klein, Chapter 8).

Stéphanie Condon (Chapter 3) focuses on the first French national survey on violence against women, which estimated the prevalence of a wide range of harmful practices, and the survey's reception by the French press and commentators. Condon is concerned with language use in methodology—in the writing of survey questions and in the description of results. She shows how her research team had to make numerous deliberate decisions about wording at multiple stages in the research process and how the findings were reported initially in the French press and then debated in public. She situates this discussion in the context of French notions of citizenship and equality and illuminates how these notions have inflected public reception of evidence of violence against women in France.

Daniela Gloor and Hanna Meier (Chapter 4) analyze official police reports on cases of domestic violence homicides in the Swiss Canton Aargau. Gloor and Meier examine how, in final case reports, police render the context of the murders in metaphorical language and thus fail to engage with the history of abuse that preceded the killings. In a British study of police files, Marianne Hester (2012) had analyzed how police represent female domestic violence perpetrators, including cases where only the woman was violent and cases where the woman and the man were violent. Analytically, Gloor and Meier focus on the use of metaphorical language in the report, which, they argue, serves as a strategy to avoid naming the abuse that occurred before the murders took place and thus obscures the gendered personal and societal contexts of the killings. In contrast, Hester (2012) had explored whether the pattern of what Michael Johnson (2008) named "intimate terrorism" fit the actions of the female perpetrators in her sample, and she concluded that it did not fit.

Anna Kwiatkowska (Chapter 5), too, focuses on domestic violence but also on sexual harassment of women by male superiors. Her empirical material includes reports in the print media and data generated in laboratory experiments. Working in Poland, her evidence concerns Polish print media and Polish attitudes toward domestic violence. Analytically, her focus is on the relationship between language use and stereotyping, which she explores in particular regarding the implications of abstract language. Within this analytical framework she shows how the use of abstract language supports stereotypical, and possibly self-serving, portrayals of victims and perpetrators.

Carole Wright and Jeff Hearn (Chapter 2) examine violence discourses in the United Kingdom. They trace definitions and uses of the word *violence* through British policy debates and discuss the implications of these uses, in particular for understanding domestic violence, in the context of wider issues of feminism, gender neutrality, and resistance against violence. Wright and Hearn then focus on the use of terms such as *gender neutrality* and *domestic violence* in the language of men who participated, either as professionals or as activists, in antiviolence efforts.

Also focusing on domestic violence and gender-neutral language, Bo Wagner Sørensen (Chapter 6) examines the naming in Denmark of interventions in perpetration. He critiques the use for perpetrator programs of the word *treatment* and its medical connotations and situates this discussion within current Danish discourses on gender equality, violence, and the state's duty to care for its citizens. In these discourses, he argues, the practice of using gender-neutral terms (such as removing references to male perpetrators) is lauded as a reflection of gender equality, although it glosses over the reality of gender-specific patterns and problems.

Also in Denmark but focusing on different patterns of abuse, Britta Mogensen (Chapter 7) examines how Danish authorities have struggled to understand and address so-called honor killings in Denmark (and Sweden), mostly of young women. Her analysis illustrates confusion among authorities over the meaning of terms such as *arranged marriage, forced marriage,* and *honor,* and a profound lack of understanding of the interpersonal dynamics in families who adhere to honor-based precepts. Citing from the published literature and her own research notes, Mogensen illuminates naïveté regarding these matters among Danish (and Swedish) authorities and the grave implications of such naïveté for young women and men whose families turn against them. Both Mogensen and Gloor and Meier, although analyzing different evidence in different countries, show how even when criminal acts against women are spoken and written about, the seriousness of these crimes and their societal significance can be downplayed or ignored.

Renate Klein (Chapter 8) takes up the distinction made previously between language for knowledge, awareness, and institutional change. Focusing on higher education in the United States, she examines language use and institutional efforts to address sexual and domestic violence on campus. Using a case example, Klein argues that language, if it is to initiate critical institutional change, needs to move beyond slogans and pledges. While positive visions are important, changes to institutional policies and workforce development require mundane procedural language issued by university management about routine institutional practice so that sexual and domestic violence is not merely implored about but addressed as systematically as environmental health and safety.

Language and Meaning: Purpose, Translation, Metaphor

While the contributions to this book reflect different research approaches, they all address the relationship between language and meaning. This relationship will be considered here from three different perspectives: purpose, translation, and metaphor. First, the notion of "purpose" of language is used to explore what is to be achieved by phrasing things a certain way. Three purposes are distinguished here: Language for knowledge refers to how language shapes insight into the nature of sexual and domestic abuse. Language for awareness refers to the role of language in creating public awareness of abuse as a widespread and serious social problem. Language for institutional change refers to what leadership and management need to say to initiate critical changes such as training the workforce in early intervention. Second, the notion of translation is used to explore practices in which language is rendered for different linguistic and cultural contexts as in translation and interpretation. All chapters in this book are in English, but not all the research represented here was generated in English. The original language contexts are Danish, English, French, German, and Polish. While each chapter focuses on language use within a particular linguistic and cultural context, the book as a whole also represents an exercise in translation and adaptation across such contexts. Hence issues of cross-context language use, and the processes in which ideas are rendered for other contexts, need to be acknowledged. Third, the use of metaphorical language is most obvious in the chapter by Gloor and Meier, but metaphor also appears in Sørensen (*treatment*, borrowed from the health field). Hence the old argument is revisited that metaphors structure human thought and action (Lakoff and Johnson 2003), and implications of this argument for framing sexual and domestic violence are suggested. In the remainder of this introduction these themes are sketched out briefly.

Purpose: Language for Knowledge, Awareness, and Institutional Change

Even though *knowledge* and *awareness* may be used interchangeably, it is argued here that the two words denote different concepts. Awareness that something is a problem does not automatically imply insight into its nature or knowledge of solutions. Many people probably are aware of numerous social and political problems around the globe without necessarily having deeper insight into the particulars of these problems or what to do about them. Furthermore, language particularly suited for one of the three purposes may not be suited for any of the others. Instead, different kinds of language may be needed so that each may "speak" most suitably to the task at hand: language for articulating what exactly it is about abusive dynamics that makes them so harmful and difficult to deal with; language for alerting the wider public to the seriousness and pervasiveness of sexual and domestic violence; and language for identifying, initiating, and implementing changes to institutional policies and practices that transform institutions into settings in which perpetration of abuse becomes less likely and support for victims more forthcoming.

Language for knowledge has been a cornerstone in the development of the field. The naming of rape and domestic violence emerged as a topic of debate in the 1970s, when feminist scholars and activists began to pro-test the use of euphemisms such as domestic disturbance and conjugal rights (Donat and D'Emilio 1992; Kelly 1988). The key emphasis of femi-nist arguments has been that sexual and domestic violence by men against women is possible and more likely if severe structural power imbalances exist (by virtue of tradition, ideology, law, religious teaching, organiza-tional hierarchy, economic inequality, or other factors) that enable men to take advantage of, exploit, and ill-treat the women in their families and intimate relationships. Ill treatment needs to be named as such and not glossed over with arcane legal terms or evasive metaphors. Catherine Kirkwood (1993), among others, emphasized the "need for a language of abuse," because abused women felt at a loss for the right words to explain to others how and why their relationships were abusive and not just going through a "normal" rough patch that every relationship experiences. Since then, notions of power and control have become almost commonplace in the field (Pence and Paymar 1993). They also have been refined consid-erably in terms of intersecting societal power inequalities (Sokoloff and Pratt 2005; Thiara, Condon, and Schröttle 2011) and gendered power in intimate relationships (Stark 2007; Johnson 2008). Although language for knowledge has been refined considerably, it remains a work in progress. In many societies, sexual and domestic violence are debated in public and moved higher on policy agendas. However, glossing over the seriousness of abuse continues—for instance, when harmful practices are excused in the name of culture.

Language for awareness, as understood here, has focused on alerting the public (and the authorities) to the fact that sexual and domestic violence are serious, widespread, and in need of societal attention. Public awareness campaigns also let victims know that their plight is recognized and that they are not alone, and campaign materials may publicize resources such as the phone numbers of help lines. For these reasons awareness cam-paigns are critically important. Two well-respected and long-running examples are Zero Tolerance, the key slogan and name of a Scottish charity[1] (Hanmer and Itzin 2000), and There's No Excuse for Domestic Violence, a campaign produced by Futures without Violence, formerly the Family Violence Prevention Fund in the United States.[2] Both campaigns are informed by considerable insight into abusive dynamics and both use memorable slogans. In terms of sheer visibility the display of campaign slo-gans in public space (in advertisements, on posters, or on bumper stickers) obviously reflects and expands public awareness that there is something wrong with domestic violence.

However, the reception of slogans is out of the hands of campaign organizers, and once such language is in circulation new problems can arise. One of these is that noble slogans are exploited for lip service by decision makers in public pronouncements, while discriminatory practices continue. Also problematic is that appeals to take sexual and domestic violence seriously appear to work "best" when examples of extreme brutality are used. The association of the words rape or domestic violence with stories of extreme abuse is noteworthy in three ways. First of all, cases of extreme abuse are in most need of help, and documenting them has been crucial for expanding victim services and changing legislation. Second, the extreme case approach is indicative of how difficult it is to have women's experiences taken seriously in societal contexts that dismiss any but the worst of treatment ("killing them is going too far" as a police officer said to a researcher in Britain; Hanmer, personal communication). Third, this creates a dilemma for campaigners, as the very messages that grab attention and may shame authorities into action may also reinforce a form of awareness in which only the worst is taken seriously and the less awful is dismissed (Wilcox 2006).

Finally, language for institutional change, as understood here, is language used by management and institutional leadership to initiate institutional transformations aimed at making perpetration of abuse more difficult and victim support easier. Institutions may (and do) use language for knowledge and for awareness in statements of commitment and preambles to institutional policies, but changes to an institution's operating procedures, its budget allocations, and its workforce development are made in the language of managerial directives. In these, institutional managers need to use the language needed, for instance, to allocate organizational funds to hire a specialist trainer from the local rape crisis center or domestic violence project, give employees leave to attend training, and require that they do so.

Marilyn Frye (1983) argued that the language and vocabulary of those who have social and institutional power is the language of consequence: what they say will be heard, what they do not say will remain taboo, and the labels they use will be the labels that stick. "Language of consequence" is not merely a matter of having high-profile individuals deliver awareness messages; it is also a matter of institutional power holders using language necessary within their respective organizations to change institutional practices.

Translation: Rendering Meaning across Linguistic and Cultural Contexts

In a cross-cultural and international field, meaning needs to be rendered in multiple languages. Where interpretation and translation are officially required, as in conferences or official publications by entities such as the European Union, the Council of Europe, or the United Nations, the need (and financial cost) of rendering meaning across linguistic contexts are particularly visible. However, even when a lingua franca is used and formal translation or interpretation are not used, all those for whom this shared language is not their native language are constantly engaging in processes of rendering meaning across languages. Yet, within much research on sexual and domestic violence, this rendering has been treated as a side issue rather than a critical phase of sense making. This is a startling omission, because without translation of some kind, international collaborative working remains profoundly limited.

The European context offers one example of the need for translation and interpretation. Since the early 1990s collaboration among scholars and practitioners from different European countries has increased dramatically—a development facilitated by the opening and integration of Europe after the fall of the Berlin Wall and reflected in a significant increase in the number of international conferences on violence against women (Logar 2011). In addition, research and development funding through the European Commission called for and enabled multicountry projects, of which some have comprised project partners from dozens of different language backgrounds.[3] The need for rendering meaning in different languages, whether done by individual researchers or professional translators, has been both intense and almost completely ignored as an element of meaning making and knowledge creation.

On one hand, this approach seems to have worked well enough, as the lively international networking and the growing multicountry project literature suggest. On the other, it is unclear how well it has worked and what may have been lost or gained in the process. Translation and interpretation can consume significant time and energy and become costly when provided by professionals. As research projects rarely have sufficient funds for such services and operate under tight deadlines, there is pressure to get on with it and hope for the best. As a result, in this field, rendering of meaning into another language has rarely been addressed as a conceptual issue or social practice.

In quantitative survey research, translation is necessary when populations are to be surveyed who speak different languages, whether within the same country or in different countries. Here, back translation is a common technique to determine the adequacy of translated items and questions (see Pearce et al., 2003, for domestic violence questionnaires). This process can make diverging connotations and subtleties of use visible where the dictionary appears to offer equivalent words (Jacquier, Fisher, and Killias 2006; Schröttle et al. 2006).

Sherry Hamby, Kaki Nix, Jacqueline De Puy, and Sylvie Monnier (2012) evaluated the use in Francophone Switzerland of a dating violence prevention program developed in the United States. This research involved focus groups with French-speaking Swiss youth on how dating relationships, abuse, sexual assault, and helping among friends are understood. The original curriculum is in English, and in addition, some of the cultural practices and images it refers to are unique to the United States. In adapting the curriculum, the American "pom-pom girl" (cheerleader waving pom-poms during a cheering routine) became a Swiss figure skater, and 16-year-olds took the bus instead of driving cars. Further ambiguity of meaning emerged in the focus group discussions, including the lack of a Swiss word carrying the connotations of *dating*. Swiss youth discussed variations of *sortir* (going out), as well as *sortir avec* (going steady), *se frequenter* (hanging out), and *flirter* (flirting). More nuances and complexities emerged with regard to the words *boyfriend* and *girlfriend*, where the French *copain* is not necessarily a date but could be a buddy, and where French slang words might be inappropriate. Overall, issues of adaptation ranged from the connotations of words to use, to the format of the curriculum and cultural underpinnings of the very notion of prevention.

With regard to translation in qualitative cross-cultural fieldwork, Kate Maclean (2007) offers a more in-depth analysis. She extends to cross-cultural translation arguments from feminist research methodology about the ethics of selecting and interpreting statements of research participants and the associated problem of "speaking for" research participants (and potentially misrepresenting what they meant; Borland 1999; Kirsch 1999). One strategy to address this problem is to invite participants to read and comment on final research reports or manuscripts. This process, if useful at all, assumes that participants are literate and have sufficient command of the language of the final outputs. When findings are published in languages the original research participants cannot understand, then participants cannot determine to what extent their intended meanings are adequately rendered in the new language. Maclean (2007) is concerned in particular with hegemonic representations of the "other" in translated research. She draws on fieldwork with an Andean population who speak Aymara and subsequent translation of fieldwork data into Spanish and English. Maclean argues that the process of translation (when given adequate attention) may help deconstruct Western terms such as *citizenship*. According to Maclean the English *citizenship* has different connotations than the Spanish *ciudadanía*, and Aymara has no such word. In a sense, the participants never spoke of "citizenship," but English speaking audiences interpret whatever was originally said in terms of "citizenship."

Thus what may look like "the same" text may be the result of shoehorning cultural nuances into the linguistic mold of another language, the fit of which may be unclear (Wierzbicka 1997 undertook detailed studies of the relationship between language, emotion, and culture). Translating the book *Our Bodies/Ourselves* required, in the words of Davis (2002: 243), "rearticulation and recontextualization."

Another matter related to "rendering meaning" that is important in the work against abuse is the need to "translate" abstract concepts into concrete action. Conny Roggeband (2004) argued that although "a global vision [of sexual violence as a universal problem] appears to facilitate the international spread of ideas and practices . . . it is unclear how activists deal with the differences . . . between their local context and the context of the activists who inspired them" (160). Roggeband (2004) offered an empirical examination of adaptation across linguistic and cultural contexts of feminist action against sexual violence. Her guiding question was whether activists "really do 'the same thing'" (159) when they take up strategies developed abroad and recreate them in their own countries (in a similar vein, Merry, 2005, noted that international human rights law needs to be "translated into the vernacular"—that is, adapted to local circumstances in order to be meaningful).

Analyzing oral history interviews and written documents (such as papers, leaflets, and meeting minutes) from Dutch and Spanish feminist organizations who were inspired by strategies developed in Britain and the United States, Roggeband concluded that early adapters do more of the same thing whereas late adapters do less of the same (and develop more modifications and variations). For both groups Roggeband stresses that what is sometimes referred to in the study of social movements as cross-national diffusion is a more active process than the term *diffusion* suggests. Rather than adopting something as it is, the process involves "interpreting, translating, and adapting" (162). Early adapters, Roggeband suggests, had fewer models (or only one) available and forged close links with the individuals who pioneered these models, resulting in strategies that were closer to the original than strategies of late adapters who could choose from among a variety of models (which by then had developed). Roggeband concludes that diffusion theories are "not adequate to explain the complex nature of intercultural communication. No attention is paid to problems of interpretation and translation" (160).

Lu Zhang (2009) undertook similar research in China in regard to a Chinese women's nongovernmental organization, the Domestic Violence Network. Using interviews, document analysis, and ethnographic observation, Zhang examines how the "transnational feminist movement's gender perspective and human rights rhetoric have been engaged, transmitted and transformed in local discourses and social policies in the context of DVN's activism" (228). Zhang finds that engaging the state, in particular the All China Women's Federation, is a double-edged sword. While advancing the cause by increasing political clout, engaging the state also "dilutes" the conceptual and political framework of gender inequality and women's human rights (237).

Several chapters in this book illuminate some of these challenges. Offering a detailed explanation of Turkish and Arabic words for honor, Mogensen shows how Danish policy and public opinion has struggled (and often failed) to grasp the connotations of these concepts and the full social significance of the practices they denote. Condon shows how French notions of gender, equality, and citizenship have influenced the methodology of a French national survey on violence against women and how they have shaped public debate of the findings. Kwiatkowska explores a social psychological model of language use, social identity, and stereotyping that was developed in English but has been employed with samples of speakers of other languages, including with Polish speakers in her research. Although the model may be applicable in several languages, its assumptions about when people prefer more abstract over more concrete language do not bear out equally across the languages tested.

Additional examples of ambiguous word use emerged in the study circle process. In translation from English to German (and vice versa), *crime* is often rendered as *Verbrechen*, but the cultural and legal connotations of the two words differ. *Crime* has stronger legal connotations, whereas *Verbrechen* has stronger moral connotations. An important concept in German-language research on violence is "Gewalt im sozialen Nahraum" (Godenzi 1996; Brandstetter 2009)—literally, violence in social near-space. The concept deliberately emphasizes proximity over blood relations or marital status in order to avoid cultural connotations of parental or conjugal rights that might be used to explain or justify sexual or domestic violence or violence against children. According to the examples posted on a translators' website, "sozialer Nahraum" has been rendered in English as "social circle," "family context," "intimate relationships," "close social circle," "intimate social environment," "immediate social proximity," "daily social aspects of the immediate environment," "close social environment," and "social setting."[4] A final example concerns names for the concept and practice of victim support centers, criminal justice agencies, and others working together to address sexual and domestic violence. Emerging in the 1990s, this practice has been called coordinated community response in the United States, multiagency work in the United Kingdom, and round table in Germany. Coordinated community response and multiagency work are relatively descriptive of the practice, whereas round table is a metaphor (see next section) borrowed from a specific episode of European politics in the late twentieth century. The original round table to this metaphor was the table around which Polish dissidents, the Solidarność-led opposition, and the Polish government came together in spring 1989 for talks on governance for post-Soviet Poland. Round table as metaphor has become shorthand for a political process in which different political factions come together for talks on how to restructure aspects of governance.

Metaphor: Borrowing Vocabulary from Other Practices

George Lakoff and Mark Johnson (2003) argue that our "ordinary conceptual system, in terms of which we both think and act, is fundamentally metaphorical in nature" (3). They note first that metaphors are pervasive in everyday language (presumably that refers not only to English) and then go on to argue that metaphors are not merely decorative elements of speech but rather central in the creation of meaning because they structure language, thought, and action.

Metaphor is defined as "the application of a word or phrase to an object or concept it does not literally denote, in order to suggest comparison with another object or concept" (Random House College Dictionary 1975). Metaphors are instances in which words or phrases that literally denote one area of experience or practice are used to denote another area of experience or practice. When using metaphorical language, vocabulary from one area is "borrowed" to describe or explain another area.

Using the example of war metaphors to describe arguments (e.g., your claims are indefensible; he shot down all my arguments) Lakoff and Johnson say that "we don't just *talk* about arguments in terms of war. We can actually win or lose arguments. . . . gain and lose ground. . . . It is in this sense that the ARGUMENT IS WAR metaphor is one that we live by in this culture [United States]; it structures the actions we perform in arguing" (4; emphasis in the original). Alternatively,

> [i]magine a culture where an argument is viewed as a dance, the participants are seen as performers, and the goal is to perform in a balanced and aesthetically pleasing way. In such a culture, people would view arguments differently, experience them differently, carry them out differently, and talk about them differently. But *we* would probably not view them as arguing at all: they would simply be doing something different. It would seem strange even to call what they were doing "arguing." . . . *The essence of metaphor is understanding and experiencing one kind of thing in terms of another.* It is not that arguments are a subspecies of war. Arguments and wars are different kings of things. (5; emphasis in the original)

As our conceptual system, according to Lakoff and Johnson, is integral to how we understand reality, metaphors (by way of influencing the conceptual system) are integral to how we understand reality, so that "what we experience, and what we do every day is very much a matter of metaphor" (3).

This approach opens an interesting vista on the role of metaphor in language for knowledge, awareness, and institutional change. Gloor and Meier offer an example of how metaphorical language can obfuscate abusive practices. They note that Swiss police in final reports of domestic violence homicides described the relationships in which the killings occurred in terms of unsettled weather ("clouds darkening the marital sky"). In using this metaphorical language, the reports (and presumably the people who wrote them) avoid a deeper understanding of the history of domestic abuse that had preceded the killings. However, metaphorical language need not always minimize abuse but may emphasize its seriousness, as in the metaphor of "intimate terrorism" (Johnson 2008). In the analysis by

Sørensen, which refers to the notion of "treatment" of domestic abusers, Danish professionals use a metaphor borrowed from medical practice for debates about political practices in gender relations and the relationship between the individual and the state.

Metaphors are common in discourses on violence against women. They can be particularly powerful in language for awareness, as the subsequent examples show. However, what makes them powerful here may limit their usefulness elsewhere. For instance, in the United States, politicians have referred to the "scourge" of domestic violence. A scourge, literally, is a whip or lash used to punish people, including self-inflicted punishment in religiously motivated penitence. *Scourge* has further religious overtones by invoking punishment for humanity sent from higher realms. It also evokes medieval drama, like the plague. Is the scourge metaphor useful language for talking about domestic violence? It may be useful for drawing attention and perhaps evoking a fleeting shudder. The scourge metaphor is not useful for structural change, however, as it does not guide pragmatic institutional action.

Another example, this one also from the United States but in terms of intervention in violence against women, concerns terms such as *combating* (intervention as warfare) and *eradicating* (intervention as pest control). Both terms metaphorically treat violence against women as an outside irritant that intrudes on but is separate from the human relationships in which the abuses occur. Both terms also evoke ruthless toughness against the intruder. But are they useful for intervention? Like the term *scourge*, *combating* and *eradicating* are dramatic and may be useful for getting attention. Unlike *scourge*, they refer to modern practices currently in use (in the United States) and thus perhaps sound more relevant (something the country does in other contexts where real wars are waged and real pests are eradicated). However, the warfare and pest-control metaphors do little for knowledge or change. They obscure the fact that domestic and sexual violence against women are woven into women's intimate and family relationships and enacted not by enemies and pests but, to a large extent, by intimates and family members. The police do not go into a home and eradicate the perpetrator. This sort of metaphorical language constructs intervention in violence against women as needing extreme measures, but the very measures invoked (warfare and pest control) are unsuited to actual intervention. Indeed, such metaphors may be counterproductive if they keep intervention locked in concepts and practices that are not applicable in reality. By using language borrowed from practices the actual use of which is virtually ruled out, language for realistic change making remains unexplored (see Klein, this volume).

The issue is not merely one of aggressive language but of how metaphorical language informs or guides actual behavior. John Paul Lederach (1991) contrasted confrontational conflict management discourses in the United States with nonconfrontational "net mending" metaphors he observed in the conversations of a family in a fishing village in Central America. Family members discussed problems in the family in terms of a broken, entangled fishing net, which needed careful and slow disentangling and repair. Although this is a refreshing alternative to metaphors of brute force, the net metaphor still requires translation into pragmatic action, because the family is not literally a net and can only metaphorically be disentangled. This again leaves open how exactly relationships among family members are "disentangled" in practice, and the question remains if and how behavior shaped by aggressive metaphors differs from behavior shaped by gentle metaphors.

A field that has considerable policy and political implications, and is increasingly multicultural and international, needs to consider the purpose of language, the rendering of meaning across linguistic and cultural contexts, and the implications of borrowing language from potentially ill-suited areas of practice. Words are not "only words" (MacKinnon 1993), nor do they necessarily do justice to their purpose. Situating each chapter in its respective national and disciplinary contexts, the contributors explore these issues from different methodological and national perspectives. It is hoped that the significance of language use, and the challenges of communicating across cultural and linguistic contexts, will come to the fore.

References

Borland, K. (1999). "'That's Not What I Said': Interpretive Conflict in Oral Narrative Research." In S. B. Gluck and D. Pata (eds.), *Women's Words: The Feminist Practice of Oral History*, 63–75. New York: Routledge.

Brandstetter, M. (2009). *Gewalt im sozialen Nahraum*. Wiesbaden: Verlag für Sozialwissenschaft.

Davis, K. (2002). "Feminist Body/Politics as World Traveler: Translating Our Bodies, Ourselves." *European Journal of Women's Studies* 9 (3): 223–47.

Donat, P. L. N., and J. D'Emilio. (1992). "A Feminist Redefinition of Rape and Sexual Assault: Historical Foundations and Change." *Journal of Social Issues* 48 (1): 9–22.

Frye, M. (1983). *The Politics of Reality: Essays in Feminist Theory.* New York: Crossing Press.

Godenzi, A. (1996). *Gewalt im sozialen Nahraum.* Basel: Helbing and Lichtenhahn.

Hamby, S., K. Nix, J. De Puy, and S. Monnier. (2012). "Adapting Dating Violence Prevention to Francophone Switzerland: A Story of Intra-Western Cultural Differences." *Violence and Victims* 27 (1): 33–42.

Hanmer, J., and C. Itzin. (2000). *Home Truths about Domestic Violence: Feminist Influences on Policy and Practice: A Reader.* London: Routledge.

Hester, M. (2012). "Portrayal of Women as Intimate Partner Domestic Violence Perpetrators." *Violence against Women* 18 (9): 1067–82.

Jacquier, V., B. S. Fisher, and M. Killias. (2006). "Cross-National Survey Designs: Equating the National Violence against Women Survey and the Swiss International Violence against Women Survey." *Journal of Contemporary Criminal Justice* 22 (2): 90–112.

Johnson, M. P. (2008). *A Typology of Domestic Violence: Intimate Terrorism, Violent Resistance, and Situational Couple Violence.* Boston: Northeastern University Press.

Kelly, L. (1988). "How Women Define Their Experiences of Violence." In K. Yllö and M. Bograd (eds.), *Feminist Perspectives on Wife Abuse,* 114–32. Thousand Oaks, CA: Sage.

Kirkwood, C. (1993). *Leaving Abusive Partners.* London: Sage.

Kirsch, G. E. (1999). *Ethical Dilemmas in Feminist Research: The Politics of Location, Interpretation, and Publication.* Albany: State University of New York Press.

Lakoff, G., and M. Johnson. (2003). *Metaphors We Live By.* Chicago: University of Chicago Press.

Lederach, J. P. (1991). "Of Nets, Nails, and Problems: The Folk Language of Conflict Resolution in a Central American Setting." In K. Avruch, P. W. Black, and J. A. Scimecca (eds.), *Conflict Resolution: Cross-Cultural Perspectives,* 165–86. Westport, CT: Greenwood Press.

Logar, R. (2011). "Violence against Women: Still a Political Problem throughout Europe." In R. K. Thiara, S. A. Condon, and M. Schröttle (eds.), *Violence against Women and Ethnicity: Commonalities and Differences across Europe*, 35–58. Opladen: Barbara Budrich Publishers.

MacKinnon, C. A. (1993). *Only Words*. Cambridge, MA: Harvard University Press.

Maclean, K. (2007). "Translation in Cross-Cultural Research: An Example from Bolivia." *Development in Practice* 17 (6): 784–90.

Merry, S. E. (2005). *Human Rights and Gender Violence: Translating International Law into Local Justice*. Chicago: University of Chicago Press.

Pearce, C. W., J. W. Hawkins, M. Kearney, C. E. Peyton, J. Dwyer, L. A. Haggerty, L. P. Higgins, B. H. Munro, U. Kelly, S. E. Toscano, C. S. Aber, D. Mahony, and M. C. Bell. (2003). "Translation of Domestic Violence Instruments for Use in Research." *Violence against Women* 9 (7): 859–78.

Pence, E., and M. Paymar. (1993). *Education Groups for Men Who Batter: The Duluth Model*. New York: Springer.

Random House College Dictionary. (1975). New York: Random House.

Roggeband, C. (2004). "'Immediately I Thought We Should Do the Same Thing': International Inspiration and Exchange in Feminist Action against Sexual Violence." *European Journal of Women's Studies* 11 (2): 159–75.

Schröttle, M., M. Martinez, S. Condon, M. Jaspard, M. Piispa, J. Westerstrand, J. Reingardiene, M. Springer-Kremser, C. Hagemann-White, P. Brzank, C. May-Chahal, and B. Penhale. (2006). "Comparative Reanalysis of Prevalence of Violence against Women and Health Impact Data in Europe— Obstacles and Possible Solutions." Coordination Action on Human Rights Violations, University of Osnabrück, Germany. Accessed August 23, 2012. http://www.cahrv.uni-osnabrueck.de/reddot/D_20_Comparative _reanalysis_of_prevalence_of_violence_pub.pdf.

Sokoloff, N. J., and C. Pratt. (2005). *Domestic Violence at the Margins: Readings on Race, Class, Gender and Culture*. New Brunswick, NJ: Rutgers University Press.

Stark, E. (2007). *Coercive Control: The Entrapment of Women in Personal Life*. New York: Oxford University Press.

Thiara, R. K., S. A. Condon, and M. Schröttle, eds. (2011). *Violence against Women and Ethnicity: Commonalities and Differences across Europe*. Opladen: Barbara Budrich Publishers.

Wierzbicka, A. (1997). *Understanding Cultures through Their Key Words: English, Russian, Polish, German, and Japanese.* New York: Oxford University Press.

Wilcox, P. (2006). *Surviving Domestic Violence: Gender, Poverty and Agency.* Basingstoke, England: PalgraveMacmillan.

Zhang, L. (2009). "Domestic Violence Network in China: Translating the Transnational Concept of Violence against Women into Local Action." *Women's Studies International Forum* 32 (3): 227–39.

Notes

1. http://www.zerotolerance.org.uk (accessed January 4, 2013).
2. http://www.futureswithoutviolence.org (accessed January 4, 2013).
3. Coordination Action on Human Rights Violations, http://www.cahrv.uni-osnabrueck.de (accessed August 22, 2012); Women Against Violence Europe network, http://www.wave-network.org (accessed August 22, 2012).
4. Linguee, http://www.linguee.de/deutsch-englisch/uebersetzung/sozialen+nahraum+.html (accessed February 26, 2013).

2

Neutralizing Gendered Violence

Subsuming Men's Violence against Women into Gender-Neutral Language

Carole Wright, United Kingdom, and
Jeff Hearn, United Kingdom/Finland

Introduction

Violence is an important but awkward word. Specifically, definitions and terms used to describe violence, and men's violence against women and children, are political. They are also often a starting point for the representation of and responses to the problem. Definitions and terms provide guides and parameters in discourses on what may, or may not, be considered, or highlighted, in policy and practice. For these reasons the politics of naming of violence and differentiating different "types" of violence bring many challenges and problems. We address the naming of such violence, especially tendencies toward the narrowing of definitions of violence, and the relationship between these two issues.

In this chapter we bring together broad policy documents and debates on naming and more detailed empirical material drawn from interviews conducted by Carole Wright with 17 men who are involved with antiviolence campaigns and/or project work, either professionally or on a volunteer basis. In ideological terms, the women's movement has created new meanings of violence and widened both the understanding and the materiality of violence. In terms of the men who work on antiviolence projects and campaigns, the ways in which they understand and talk about violence, along with the ways in which these understandings are translated into men's antiviolence programs, denote the furthering of the ideas of the women's movement, the redressing of injustice, and the policies with which to do this, albeit in an institutionalized setting and within their own subjective positioning. In this way, this chapter explores feminism as a social organizer of "domestic violence." Following discussion of country context and academic background, we explore how "feminism" organizes gender-neutral definitions of "domestic violence" and the complex ways in which it influences institutions, organizations, and individuals. This includes the discourses of resistance that have arisen to counter feminist analyses of "domestic violence" and the discourses feminists have created to counter this counterresistance.

Country Context: Dynamic Contestations in the United Kingdom

Definitions are always subject to political, historical, and cultural conditions, and indeed these vary even within different parts of the United Kingdom. For example, Scottish Women's Aid has long campaigned for including gender in the definition of domestic violence and abuse. Achieving this in Scotland marked a shift in problem representation and enhanced policy development. Scottish Women's Aid has also argued that the word *abuse* better represents both the physical and psychological dimensions of domestic violence, including ongoing manipulation of power, in intimate relationships; this approach has been taken up by the Scottish Executive: "Domestic abuse (as gender-based abuse) can be perpetrated by partners or ex-partners and can include physical abuse (assault & physical attack involving a range of behaviour), sexual abuse (acts which degrade and humiliate women and are perpetrated against their will, including rape) and mental and emotional abuse (such as threats, verbal abuse, racial abuse, withholding money and other types of controlling behaviour such as isolation from family and friends)" (Scottish Executive, 2000: 5).

In the United Kingdom, current definitions reflect developing knowledge of culture and religion and now include forced marriage and so-called honor crimes, as seen in the definitions published online by Women's Aid Federation England and the overall UK government.

In Women's Aid's view domestic violence is physical, sexual, psychological or financial violence that takes place within an intimate or family-type relationship and that forms a pattern of coercive and controlling behaviour. This can include forced marriage and so-called "honour crimes." Domestic violence may include a range of abusive behaviours, not all of which are in themselves inherently "violent." (Women's Aid Federation England 2007)

Any incident of threatening behaviour, violence or abuse (psychological, physical, sexual, financial or emotional) between adults who are or have been intimate partners or family members, regardless of gender or sexuality. This includes issues of concern to black and minority ethnic (BME) communities such as so called "honour killings." (Home Office 2009)

While it is clear that feminism has influenced governmental definitions, the gender neutrality in these "official" quotes is noteworthy. Nevertheless, this gender neutrality is combated on both Women's Aid and UK government websites, as both use statistics and impart information in gender-specific terms regarding women as victims and men as perpetrators. For example, the UK government site states that 89 percent of people experiencing four or more incidents are women, and on average two women per week are killed by their current or former partner.

Another key UK organization dealing with "domestic violence" is Respect, the umbrella organization for men's perpetrator programs in "domestic violence." Their definitions of domestic violence differ slightly. One Respect website is for the Men's Advice Line, supported by the Home Office, which provides telephone help for male victims of "domestic violence." The other site is for the Respect Phoneline, providing support for women experiencing "domestic violence" and men who are being violent and/or abusive. On the former, the definition is in gender-neutral language, despite being directed at male victims. However, on the Respect Phoneline website, the initial face of the website uses gender-neutral language but also states that the majority of "domestic violence" occurs in heterosexual relationships and is committed overwhelmingly by men. The Respect Phoneline website also directs both women and men to webpages where the language denotes "domestic violence" as violence toward women by men (Respect Phoneline 2009). Clearly, there is an incongruity between the definitions of "domestic violence," which have been reconceptualized into gender-neutral language, and the ways in which these definitions are then backed up in surrounding texts, where the use of gender-specific language is prevalent.

However, these debates are contested and dynamic, and writing this now at the end of 2011, the UK government Equalities Office states, "The UK has signed the UN Convention on the Elimination of All Forms of Discrimination Against Women (CEDAW). The definition of Violence against Women and Girls (VAWG) in CEDAW is 'violence directed at a woman because she is a woman or acts of violence which are suffered disproportionately by women'" (Government Equalities Office website, no date). Having noted that, overall much of the work of this sector working against violence to women tends to emphasize women's experiences thereof, rather than men's practices of violence (Hearn and McKie 2010).

Academic Context: Feminism, Gender Neutrality, "Domestic Violence" Discourse, and Resistances

Violence may be defined from several, sometimes overlapping, standpoints: the violated, the violator, those dealing with violence, and those who observe violence (Hearn 1998). The prominence given to any one perspective (or definition) reflects the shifting nature of power. The term *domestic violence* continues to be used in many countries and Anglophone contexts, despite its shortcomings analytically. Not all "domestic violence" occurs in the home or between those sharing a home. There have been extensive critiques of the term *domestic violence* for being nongendered and for being unclear on exactly how or how not "the home" figures in that violence (see DeKeseredy and Hinch 1991; Hanmer 1998; Harne and Radford 2008). The word *domestic* and its association with home and privacy, together with an apparent ungenderedness, inadequately reflects and even diminishes the extent and nature of the problem. The alternative term *violence against women* does not directly include *violence against children*, and within that last term, *children* includes boys who grow into men and older boys who become and overlap with young men. Moreover, one thing that these examples have in common is that they mainly concern "men's violences." This is a more accurate term but is still not perfect—for example, there is violence in some lesbian relationships. A rather different issue is how men can talk about their doing of violence but also include violences done to them without excusing their own violence or treating it as parallel.

Such namings of violence, distinctions between types of violence, and conceptualizations around violence feed into public and policy discourses. For instance, a split may be made between "domestic violence" and "sexual violence" (or sexualized violence) or between "violence against women" and "child abuse." In the United Kingdom such distinctions are connected to how some local authorities and other organizations use the term *violence against women* to include all violences, while others separate different violences for different purposes, such as funding streams. Many nonstatutory agencies, especially women's groups, have argued that the word *abuse* better represents the psychological and physical dimensions of violence and helps shift emphasis from physical violence to ongoing manipulation of power in intimate relationships.

Feminist definitions of *domestic violence* are usually underpinned by analyses of unequal gendered social relations. The problem of men's violences toward women is seen to stem from men's sense of entitlement and maintenance of power and control. This sense of entitlement is associated within a context of privilege and male dominance, backed by sexism within the private and public spheres and patriarchal structures. Women have in many ways worked to widen the social understandings of violence and to bring these violences into the public sphere.

At the same time, there is often a dissonance in how people talk about "domestic violence" in their everyday lives and work. The frequent reconceptualization of "domestic violence" into a social problem that is gender neutral has been written into policy, and responses from this study show how this gender-neutral discourse is taken up, activated, reproduced, and indeed also resisted by various actors. However, before we explore this evidence, it is necessary to set out what we mean by "resistance."

The development of discourses of resistance can be understood at at least four levels: first, nonfeminist frameworks, which were prevalent in the past, particularly in police responses, where, for example, "domestic violence" is seen as "just a domestic"; second, feminist analyses of "domestic violence" that challenged nonfeminist analyses, so constituting the first discourses of resistance; third, analyses challenging feminist frameworks, such as gender-neutral analyses, which can be seen as counterdiscourses; and fourth, feminist and profeminist analyses to counter these counterdiscourses, which can be seen as counter-counterdiscourses.

Discourses of resistance can also be seen as an old struggle against violence to women that has now been reconfigured as counter-counterdiscourses in order to resist emerging rhetoric around conceptualizations of "domestic violence" as gender neutral. In direct relation to the gender-neutral discourse, working at different levels is a further public discourse, which has begun to circulate widely, whereby both women and men, when talking about "domestic violence" or men's violences, activate a discourse around women's violence toward men. This argument can be seen as a counterdiscourse. The "women are as violent as men" discourse is more commonly known in professional and academic circles as gender symmetry, and it has much to do with the "conflict tactics scales" (CTS; Straus 1979). Some studies using the CTS found that women admitted to doing as much violence as men, and thus Straus concludes that gender symmetry exists in "domestic violence." His methodology has been widely criticized by many scholars for not taking context into consideration. Questions on violence did not include meaning, motive, or outcome, and neither does the scale include sexual violence (a later version of the scale does), separation assault, stalking, or homicide (DeKeseredy and Kelly 1993; Renzetti 1994; DeKeseredy 1999; Morrow 2000; DeKeseredy and Dragiewicz 2007). When Walter DeKeseredy and Katharine Kelly (1993) adapted the CTS to include context, meaning, motive, and outcome, a substantially different picture emerged, with only a minority of women initiating attacks against their partners.

Nevertheless, the discourse of symmetry has gained much currency in recent years. Arguably, these types of discourses can be seen as resistance toward women's gender-based campaigning to stop violence against women, with much of this opposition including an antifeminist perspective. Nevertheless, the outcome of this has led some writers to argue that the single factor of gender is no longer relevant and thinking around violence against women should move beyond feminist theories (Dutton 1994; 2006; Graham-Kevan 2007). It is worth noting that most feminist writers, theorists, professionals, and activists do not shy away from or dismiss women's violence. In fact, areas of research such as same-sex violence have seen considerable growth. Most feminist writers and activists acknowledge that men can be victims of violence and have no desire to negate this. Indeed feminist women recognize that male victims of violence require support and services. Moreover, a feminist framework is well placed for analyzing and explaining much of men's violence against other men, in terms of structural systems, men as a social category, masculinity, hierarchy, and the need to prove physical prowess to other men. Feminist scholars recognize that violence is multidimensional and include intersecting factors such as race, class, age, ability, and religion. What researchers consistently find in studying women's violence, however, is that it is quantitatively and qualitatively different from men's violence. Sex and gender remain significant and relevant in the etiology of intimate or "domestic" violence (Renzetti 1994).

In order to place this type of research in perspective, it is first necessary for (pro)feminist writers to set out and in some sense reproduce the language and texts of antifeminist analysis. In this sense, through the process of resistance and critique, (pro)feminist writers may ironically activate antifeminist discourse. The next section explores further how gender-neutral discourses and the discourse of gender symmetry was used by some of the men activists interviewed.

Empirical Data

Activist Men's Use of Gender Neutrality and "Domestic Violence"

The gender-neutral discourse on "domestic violence" is generally accepted in wider society and has developed into a public discourse that helps shape consciousness, providing a new language from which to draw. The men, antiviolence professionals, and activists interviewed all defined *domestic violence* in a standardized way:[1] namely, the current definition put forward by and theorized by feminists regarding power and control. Some professional participants demonstrated their further knowledge of feminist definitions of violence against women by incorporating a continuum of violence (Kelly 1988). None of the participants proposed gender symmetry between men's and women's "domestic violence"; rather, some participants actively resisted this and bemoaned the ways that gender neutrality has worked its way into public discourse. Matthew (all names are anonymized), a campaign worker, talked about institutions, organizations, and individuals being positive toward the campaign, but he acknowledged that some people used the gender-symmetry discourse: "So, all overwhelmingly positive. I can only think of few emails from individuals erm, men who've said things like 'What about violence against men? Why aren't you doing something about this, blah, blah, blah?'"

Sean, from the same campaign, also talked about the development of new discourses around gender-neutral "domestic violence":

> **But,** there is something new happening. Now what happened, when I actually began to concretely, on the ground, began to start going round to people with materials that erm, were provided to me by the campaign to simply have that discussion with somebody, about would you carry this [campaign

symbol] . . . **This** was actually the trigger for **loads** of people of **all** ages, **males**, very tentatively discussing their experiences. And they were proud to wear the [campaign symbol] right, err and you know, but they also wanted to say that they were, that **they** were experiencing unprovoked violence and levels of aggression from you know, female people that they were in relationships with.

This illustrates how engaging in a discourse of men's violences activates the counterdiscourse of women's violence against men. Sean himself has experienced violence done to him by women and has some sympathy for what men are trying to say about women's violence. The discourse, however, appears to be only partial and not fully understood by many men: "But they had no yardstick for measuring and that they, and that they couldn't understand and erm, so young men, students at university, of 19, would, were telling me things like this, and you know, older guys trying to explain their complex things."

Most men that Sean encountered tended to be cautious, hesitant, and confused when they spoke about women's violence toward men, but Sean also experienced an accompanying hostility with this discourse: "Some people got really nasty like. You could sort of tell who were perhaps, people who, you know, had their own shame and guilt and anxiety about their own actions and things like that, and they were getting nasty about the issue. They were the ones who were saying, 'no, well, I'm not going to wear the [campaign symbol] and I'm not, you know, I don't agree with this, 'cos it's one-sided. Why should men, you know, stop being violent if women aren't stopping being violent?'"

These attitudes draw on discourses of reciprocity and injustice but also display a resistance toward feminist analyses of violence against women. The gender-symmetry discourse is invoked unproblematically, and any critique of male power is effectively avoided and/or dismissed. Another participant, Robert, was aware of the gender-neutral discourse and its location within gender-equality processes, and he believed the government used it in a calculative manner:

The "in thing," the Government's, just wants this to **look** like we're doing equality stuff here, or it's a sop to organisations like Father's for Justice. Erm, which is quite clever if it is, and Machiavellian, but actually, they know it's like, Respect aren't going to come out with stuff that say that men are terribly badly treated in society. Erm, it's like **playing** off areas, elements in the debate, against each other, erm. But then the other side of it is there is a men's agenda, there are, there are **some** men, allegedly, (laughs) who are abused by women, erm, and, you know, those, that's difficult and traumatic and some of that stuff will be hidden. It seems we learn something from women's experience of experiencing abuse, that, you know, for men to come out and stuff that will be another set of difficulties and barriers for them to come out and say: "This is happening to me!" Erm, so it's a serious issue, it's just not, it's not a majority issue.

Here Robert highlights the complex ways in which institutional responses are influenced by gender-neutral discourse, and he sees an obvious dissonance between policy and what actually happens in practice. The Respect website is one of the few that uses gendered pronouns in their definitions. Thus Robert's remark about Respect not taking up the rhetoric of gender symmetry is in line with their website text. Respect's position, then, is disseminated both to the general public who use the site and through their member organizations to such an extent that, as an individual, Robert takes up a resistance discourse. Robert acknowledges men as victims of "domestic violence" but also acknowledges that feminist frameworks are useful for addressing this, especially in overcoming barriers men might face in seeking support. Moreover, Robert brings Fathers for Justice into his analysis as an example of an antifeminist organization that uses the gender-symmetry discourse and believes that women have more rights than men, particularly regarding child custody after separation and divorce.

In Robert's extract, the concept of feminism is drawn on directly in order to acknowledge and frame the difficulties that male victims of "domestic violence" might face in coming forward, as well as accessing support. Thus "domestic violence" might also be seen as a component concept contained within feminism. In addition, Robert draws on the discourse of antifeminism via women's rights and Fathers for Justice. However, antifeminism is meaningless without an understanding of the concept of feminism. In this sense, feminism/antifeminism are constructed as binary opposites, with antifeminism relying on feminism in order to make and convey meaning. As such, antifeminism can be seen as an additional concept contained within feminism, working at various levels and in complex ways. For these participants, the gender-neutral discourse of "domestic violence" also tends to invoke the gender-specific discourse of "domestic violence." Whether the discourses are invoked in positive or negative ways, however, is not the main issue. Rather, it appears that gender-neutral discourses, because they have evolved from gender-specific discourses, rely on gender-specific discourses for meaning. Thus the gender-neutral discourse now activates the gender-specific discourse, and vice versa. The complexity involved in these back-and-forth exchanges of gender-neutral/ specific discourses gives rise to their analysis within the wider social relations that make up feminist opposition.

"Domestic Violence" and the Neutralization of Feminism

More broadly, gender-neutral discourses of "domestic violence" can be located within the wider context of resistance toward feminism—including the processes that can work to regulate "domestic violence" through institutional, organizational, and individual practices—and thus hide and/or subsume feminism and the feminist struggle. Resistance, or counterdiscourses, toward gender-based, feminist analyses on "domestic violence" can also be seen as constituting part of the wider picture of resistance or "backlash" against feminism itself (Renzetti 1994). To open up the undermining of feminist analyses of "domestic violence," it is necessary to locate it in a context of wider hostilities toward feminism. A common term for locating the different forms of resistance to feminism and feminist theory is *backlash*. While the term *backlash* is subject to critique, there are few alternative terms that incorporate the complexities of different forms and levels of resistance.

It is on account of feminist women that a huge body of research and service provision now exists around "domestic violence." While it is unremarkable that the Home Office website does not mention feminism, it is perhaps more surprising that neither Women's Aid Federation England nor Respect present themselves as feminist or profeminist organizations. Clearly Respect's definitions of violence are underpinned by feminist theory and feminist thinking, and the Women's Aid website is saturated with feminist references and research. Women's Aid England advertises itself as "the key national charity working to end domestic violence against women and children" (Women's Aid Federation England 2009). Yet there is no explicit mention of their feminist ethos. This is in contrast to, for example, Rape Crisis England and Wales, who support local Rape Crisis Centres and work to eliminate all forms of sexual violence. Rape Crisis states very clearly on their website that they "are a feminist organisation." All three

NEUTRALIZING GENDERED VIOLENCE   31

of these institutions and organizations are talking about violence against women, yet only one states its feminist ethos publicly.

Following earlier comments on diversity in the United Kingdom and looking more closely at Women's Aid, there are marked differences across the England, Wales, Scotland, Northern Ireland, and (Southern) Ireland websites, reflecting the diversity already noted. Only Ireland and Wales state clearly on their website home pages that they are feminist organizations: "Women's Aid is a feminist, political and campaigning organisation committed to the elimination of violence and abuse of women through effecting political, cultural and social change" (Women's Aid, Ireland 2009). "The logo reflects our key principles, that we are a feminist organisation, run by women for women" (Welsh Women's Aid 2009). At first glance, it may appear unimportant that England, Scotland, and Northern Ireland choose not to mention feminism. However, all three accompanying website texts belie this choice by using statements that are clearly feminist in their origination. For example, Women's Aid Federation England states on their website: "Domestic violence is a violation of women and children's human rights. It's the result of an abuse of power and control, and is rooted in the historical status of women in the family and in society" (Women's Aid Federation England 2009). Regarding women's historical oppression through men's dominance strongly suggests that they are feminist organizations, but it would appear that women's organizations have had to invent new strategies and ways of showing their feminist ethos without actually referring to the word *feminist*.

Tensions lay in "feminism as political." To many activist women, being "feminist" is a political statement, in the sense that *feminist* is saturated with meaning, ideas, beliefs, and strategies to further the struggle in alleviating women's oppression. Although the ideologies associated with feminism are not unified, retaining this political status is important for many women, as it affirms feminism as a social movement and motivates women in a negative neoliberal climate that effectively suppresses much activism around women's rights. Indeed, the mainstreaming of activists into standardized working practices can dilute a movement's political edge. This is especially true of groups who transfer themselves to charity statuses.

The act of some obviously feminist organizations not stating publicly their feminist ethos indicates that "feminism" is akin to what Dorothy Smith (1999) calls an "ideological code," which socially organizes how some focus of interest—in this specific context, violence against women—can be expressed. Their counterdiscourses of resistance to this, however, are clear in their accompanying texts, which use feminist language and are gender specific. It is also important to note that although "political" constitutes a component part within the feminist code, its status is ambiguous. Both Women's Aid Federation and Rape Crisis England and Wales are feminist organizations, at least in their ethos and origination, and both hold charity status. In this sense, the question arises as to whether or not their decision to publicly state their feminist criteria has an impact on their political activism around violence against women and in what ways this might influence the type of political activity they engage in. The next section explores further how feminism is masked and/or subsumed at the level of campaigns, organizations, and individuals.

Subsuming Feminism: Campaigns and Men's Group-Work Programs

This analysis is based on a section of the interviews that asked practitioners and activist men to discuss their everyday work. They were asked to keep in mind such things as feminist protocols, funding, employment, employment criteria, and recordkeeping. Their responses reveal the complexities of how "feminism" organizes the ways in which violence is talked about and disseminated within the men's programs themselves. Most participants recognized that feminist analyses of "domestic violence" underpinned rationales for both the campaigns and the men's group-work programs. However, for most participants there was no explicit acknowledgment of this connection, as Billy, a practitioner, points out:

> Er, it's not carved in stone anywhere, erm, I think it, it comes through because, of it, for **me** because of where I've been. It, it comes out. I think if someone saw me working, or, they'd say, "yeah, that's, that's basically, that's, that's got feminist, it's informed by feminism certainly." Certainly in terms or attitude **around** violence towards women and children, er, and the way we challenge erm, I was going to say, old assumptions, that's all quite current assumptions, around, assumptions, that men **carry** around **owner**ship of women, around power over women, around women's role in society and, and in, in the home. All those things are quite, erm, robustly challenged.

Billy describes the framework used in an organization working with men, which is clearly influenced by "radical feminist" tenets. Significantly, Billy has to actively think about whether feminism underpins the group-work programs, and he brings in an unnamed other to act as objective onlooker before he can confirm that feminism does inform the men's programs. This suggests that feminism is not talked about within this particular organization, or at least not in the everyday situations that involve Billy.

For Alex, another practitioner, the funding for his organization came directly from Women's Aid, and his work coordinates with other services provided to women:

> That means that our ethos is, is likely to be feminist, because of their perspective on the way that we should do the work. So I, I might, I might have a, I, I don't have a, a different view about the work from, from them, but the way we do the work isn't, isn't determined by me alone. It's determined by the people that we're working with and how they know we should be doing the work. I think it's difficult for a man to state that you follow a f, f, a feminist perspective, but I think that the work that we do, does to that way of thinking.

For Alex, there is no question about whether the organization he works for is feminist. It is feminist because of its connection with Women's Aid, whom they work very closely with, and who oversee the operation and style of group-work programs in use. For Alex then, feminism clearly organizes the operation of "domestic violence" intervention. Nevertheless, it appears that the hiding of feminism within the group work still happens but through more complex processes. It occurs within a context of simultaneous assumption of feminism and a nervousness, or apprehension, in claiming to be feminist. He is aware of his maleness, of the social relations between men and women, and he is also aware of feminism as recourse to women's oppression.

This complexity is also demonstrated by other participants. Sam, who works in an organization that trains individuals and agencies to work with violent men, is very knowledgeable about feminism; he engages with it in his everyday life and allies himself most closely with radical feminism. Asked about his training of others and whether he employs any feminist protocol, he responds,

> So we look at theories where—those theories that kind of claim that men's violence against women is because they had a, err, they were abused as children; or because they saw dad hit mum; erm, or because of their alcohol use; or because of their drug use; or because of stress; or because of anger management; or because they had a poor relationship with mum. And err, you know so we go through all those theories with, with the delegates on the training, you know towards bringing them to the **the**ory that

we believe and that we would like them to kind of work **by**. Or obviously it's
their choice whether they do, which is that, you know men's violence against
women, erm, is rooted in their beliefs err of **r**ights over women, which is
socially em—inbuilt, embedded, and supported, erm, err for the, for the aim
of power and control. Erm, which we promote as a feminist theory. Erm, err,
but we don't promote it as **radical**, erm we don't go into different feminist
thinking, we cl—you know, but we promote it as feminist thought.

Here, Sam dispels many of the individual or pathological explanations for violence against women and actively works through some of the
prevalent discourses of resistance toward conveying feminist analyses of
"domestic violence." On the one hand, Sam works with other people in
a "training the trainers" capacity and is not afraid to use the term *feminist*; thus he can be seen as furthering the goals of the women's movement.
On the other, he outlines radical feminist tenets but consciously hides this
from those he trains and promotes it as general feminist thought. By not
referring to "radical" feminism, he attempts to overcome men's negative
constructions of feminism and feminists. Sam's promoting of radical feminist tenets as general feminism raises the possibility of mistaking radical
feminism for liberal feminism, which is tolerated more easily. Although
Sam identifies strongly with radical profeminism and incorporates it at
a practitioner level, he nevertheless demonstrates a complex process that
works to mask some feminisms.

Lewis, a campaigner, complicates feminism and its organization of
"domestic violence" further, by bringing into play the concept of human
rights:

> So yes I have been very well exposed to this by my family, p-people who are
> very dear to me who I respect the opinions of. Erm, and I have friends who
> I think would class themselves as radical feminists, erm, both straight and
> gay. Erm, now in terms of the influence of that on the campaign, I am sure
> that, err, account will be taken of feminist, erm, issues, within it. Erm, and
> that type of issue will be—come up in debate, but we would tend not to **label**
> it as feminist, erm because of the organisation is concerned with **hum**an
> rights, therefore the whole—one of the whole aims is to try to de-stereotype,
> erm, people into mm-feminine/masculine **etc.**, so it would be very much
> the approach—very much that this person is a human, erm and any form of
> inequality would be, erm frowned upon.

One point of note here is that Lewis brought up the term *radical feminist* himself. Nevertheless, Lewis says that the campaign would not "label"

itself as feminist. He also stresses the word *label* in order to separate feminism from the underlying ethos that drives the campaign, which is human rights–based. The process of actively subsuming feminism is done by arguing that men and women are people and any inequalities are unacceptable. What this does, however, is to avoid talking about power relations between men and women, and thus the forces that drive feminist activism. To compound this further, the "human rights" concept is drawn on as a reason for deconstructing masculine and feminine gender stereotypes, but the deconstructing of gender is central to feminism, especially radical forms of feminism. Thus one of the key facets of feminism is effectively "appropriated" by the human rights concept.

The next extract from Lewis, who interrupts the interviewer (C) in midsentence, exemplifies how the process of reasoned argument allows people to neatly sidestep feminism:

> C Except the campaign **does** say it's [about
>   L [Yeah, that caused a **big** debate. Erm, yeah, because a-wh-yy when the, when the debate first-when the **campaign** first started, erm, I don't know, four—what are we, 2006?—four, five years ago? The, the real **prob**lem that people had to get their heads round was "why are we campaigning for violence against women? Why aren't we campaigning ag-for violence against humans?" Erm, the reason **why** it was agreed to, was one: because 52% of humans happen to be female, therefore we are campaigning for females ah-sor-for humans who happen to be female as well; and the second aspect of it was that there were certain types of violence which were committed on women which weren't typically committed on males: domestic violence, typically rape etc., things like this, violence against men **tend** to be of a different type.

Drawing on democracy and the democratic nature of the campaign, statistics are utilized—52 percent of humans are women—to justify why a campaign regarding violence against women is acceptable to its members. This debate sets out what feminists have struggled to expose regarding violence against women, but it still manages to keep these social problems within a "human rights" discourse. Smith (1999) analyzes the function of "political correctness" and "human rights" as ideological codes and the way in which these codes translate into "public discourses." Once we learn how to "read" these codes, we can become what she calls "institutionally captured" by them. Returning to Lewis's account, "human rights" as an "ideological code" is given high legitimacy in public discourse because it is also politically correct, which, as stated, is also another ideological code and adds to an already complex network of discourses and counterdiscourses. Lewis's extracts exemplify highly complex procedures and demonstrate how the ideological codes of "politically correct" and "human rights" can complement each other and upgrade the rhetorical value of a given dilemma.

Most of the men participants are campaigning and delivering programs from a "radical feminist" framework, particularly in relation to patriarchal power. Yet most neglect to use the term *feminism* in their everyday work. The strategies Sam uses for training on "domestic violence" allow him to arrive at feminist analyses of "domestic violence" with trainees. However, despite being open about feminism, he simultaneously masks radical feminism, which points to feminism not only as regulating how "domestic violence" is talked about but also as an ideological code. Lewis demonstrated further complexities in the use of ideological codes that impact directly on campaign members. In as much as ideological codes have caused debates within the campaign, this illustrates that the codes, and the discourses contained within them, can be contradictory and constraining. Ideological codes can be used in complex ways to counter feminist ideology, and subsume it, thus acting as an additional discourse of resistance that contributes to the "backlash" or opposition toward feminism.

Discussion and Conclusion

This chapter has looked at how gender-neutral discourses of "domestic violence" have gained discursive currency, how they have provided a new rhetoric from which to draw on, and how they can work to shape consciousness. It has shown how it is possible to situate and analyze the development of gender-neutral discourses of "domestic violence" within a context of "backlash," or opposition, toward feminist analyses of violence against women. This opposition can also be situated within the wider context of resistance toward feminism, where it constitutes an important factor in a complex network of resistance, counterresistance, and counter-counterresistance. The symmetry discourse of "domestic violence" assists the gender neutrality that is now found in definitions at institutional levels. Together, these two factors play a significant role in helping to neutralize feminism. The website data from key institutions, along with data from events and participants, demonstrate how these counterdiscourses and counter-counterdiscourses are institutionally endorsed and then taken up and activated by professionals and the general public. The highly complex ways in which discourses of resistance are used have been partially unpacked in this chapter, which has uncovered some of the techniques and strategies that are used to subsume feminism, or to at least avoid using the term. Many of the men's programs appear to operate from a "radical feminist" philosophy, regarding patriarchal power and control, yet distance themselves not only from "radical feminism" but often from feminism in the more general sense.

This chapter has examined how discourses such as "human rights" carry an authority that works to downgrade feminism. Through an intricate set of processes, "human rights" discourse, though a component part of feminism, manages to grow in significance and incorporate feminism such that feminism is subsumed. When feminism is analyzed in this context, questions arise regarding the social power that men in these campaigns and organizations hold and how they are part of a wider net of social relations producing "expert" knowledge. However, this "expert" knowledge may contribute to incorporation of violence against women into institutional settings within which feminist "work" is controlled, regulated, and subsumed.

More generally, the narrowing of definitions of violence may link to further tendencies toward focusing on men's violences in isolation from other aspects of gendered power relations. In everyday accounts, policy and research seems to be a pull to the individual (man) and his individual violence. Violence is dominantly seen as owned, as individual, as in a time and place, as incidents, as aberrant. This neglects the conditions that produce or facilitate violence and the means of supporting violence, including men's relations with men. Despite its possible moral appeal, there is a problem with focusing on violence narrowly and exclusively. A paradox can be recognized between the need to focus on men's violences and the danger of separating, even isolating, violence from the rest of social life. Interestingly, the separation of violence from the rest of social life (e.g., childcare, sexuality, housework, child abuse) is a feature of many research interviews with men who have used violence against women (Hearn 1998). Even when that violence, especially certain forms of physical violence, is described explicitly and in detail, sexual(ized) violence or child abuse may be ignored. The relative isolation of violence from the rest of social life is one way that research on violence may proceed. Both these kinds of men's accounts and research itself may assist in reproducing violences. There can be a danger in researching men's violence without and outside of context, reducing "it" to a thing to be measured with relative ease. Narrowing violence to particular types of violences may include a focus on physical violence, particular types of physical violence, avoidance of sexual violence and child abuse, and avoidance of long-term, more subtle psychological and emotional violence and violation.

Violence and violation need to be seen in an open-ended way, where they are often not seen and taken for granted. Violence and violation need to be linked with other negative processes, such as oppression, exploitation, and marginalization, and sometimes even to "positive" processes, such as love, caring, support, and loyalty. *Violence* is an important and powerful word, especially if not abstracted and isolated from society, even if it is still awkward and imperfect.

References

DeKeseredy, W. S. (1999). "Tactics of the Antifeminist Backlash against Canadian National Woman Abuse Surveys." *Violence Against Women* 5 (11): 1258–76.

DeKeseredy, W. S., and M. Dragiewicz. (2007). "Understanding the Complexities of Feminist Perspectives on Woman Abuse: A Commentary on Donald G. Dutton's Rethinking Domestic Violence." *Violence Against Women* 13 (8): 874–84.

DeKeseredy, W. S., and R. Hinch. (1991). *Woman Abuse: Sociological Perspectives*. Ontario: Thompson.

DeKeseredy, W. S., and K. Kelly. (1993). "The Incidence and Prevalence of Woman Abuse in Canadian University and College Dating Relationships." *Canadian Journal of Sociology* 18: 137–59.

Dutton, D. G. (1994). "Patriarchy and Wife Assault: The Ecological Fallacy." *Violence and Victims* 9 (2): 167–82.

Dutton, D. G. (2006). *Rethinking Domestic Violence*. Vancouver: University of British Columbia Press.

Government Equalities Office. (no date). Accessed June 18, 2013. http://sta.geo.useconnect.co.uk/what_we_do/violence_against_women.aspx.

Graham-Kevan, N. (2007). "Domestic Violence Typologies." In J. Hamel and T. Nicholls (eds.), *Family Interventions in Domestic Violence: A Handbook of Gender-Inclusive Theory and Treatment*, 145–65. New York: Springer.

Hanmer, J. (1998). "Out of Control: Men, Violence and Family Life." In J. Popay, J. Hearn, and J. Edwards (eds.), *Men, Gender Divisions and Welfare*, 128–46. London: Routledge.

Harne, L., and J. Radford. (2008). *Tackling Domestic Violence: Theories, Policies and Practice*. Maidenhead: McGraw-Hill/Open University Press.

Hearn, J. (1998). *The Violences of Men*. London: Sage.

Hearn, J., and L. McKie. (2010). "Gendered and Social Hierarchies in Problem Representation and Policy Processes: 'Domestic Violence' in Finland and Scotland." *Violence Against Women* 16 (2): 136–58.

Home Office, United Kingdom. (2009). Crime Reduction, Domestic Violence Minisite. Accessed July 2009. http://www.crimereduction.homeoffice.gov.uk/dv/dv01.htm.

Kelly, L. (1988). *Surviving Sexual Violence*. Cambridge: Polity.

Morrow, M. (2000). "Research and Activism on Violence against Women: Academic Discourses for the New Millennium." *Critical Criminology* 9 (1/2): 153–62.

Renzetti, C. M. (1994). "On Dancing with a Bear: Reflections on Some of the Current Debates among Domestic Violence Theorists." *Violence and Victims* 9 (2): 195–200.

Respect Phoneline. (2009). "The Truth about Domestic Violence." Accessed July 2009. http://www.respect.uk.net/pages/the-truth-about-domestic-violence.html.

Respect Phoneline. (2009). "What Is Abuse?" Accessed July 2009. http://www.respectphoneline.org.uk/pages/what-is-abuse.html.

Scottish Executive. (2000). *National Strategy to Address Domestic Abuse in Scotland*. Edinburgh: Stationery Office.

Smith, D. E. (1999). *Writing the Social: Critique, Theory, and Investigations*. Toronto: University of Toronto Press.

Straus, M. A. (1979). "Measuring Intrafamily Conflict and Violence: The Conflict Tactics (CT) Scales." *Journal of Marriage and the Family* 41: 75–88.

Welsh Women's Aid. (2009). Accessed July 2009. http://welshwomensaid.org.uk.

Women's Aid, Ireland. (2009). "Mission Statement." Accessed July 2009. http://www.womensaid.ie/about/mission.html.

Women's Aid Federation of England. (2007). "*What Is Domestic Violence?*" Accessed July 2009. http://www.womensaid.org.uk/domestic-violence -articles.asp?section=00010001002200410001&itemid=1272.

Women's Aid Federation of England. (2009). "*What We Believe.*" Accessed July 2009. http://womensaid.org.uk/page.asp?section=00010001000190002 &sectionTitle=What+we+believe.

Note

1. Note, the bold typeface in all quotations denotes the emphasis used by participants to stress certain words, or syllables in a word, during the course of their interviews.

3

Communicating Prevalence Survey Results

Stéphanie A. Condon, France

Over the past two decades, academics in Europe have been allocating time and funds to investigate the forms, intensity, and explanations of violence against women. This was the result of efforts of nongovernmental organizations, the feminist movement, and feminist theorists to move over to the public realm an issue whose consequences reach far beyond the private sphere to which it had previously been confined. Such surveys were also a recommendation of the Beijing Platform, given that the issue could not be adequately addressed using existing data from administrative or legal sources. Thus we have seen large-scale collection of empirical data, in order to address what has come to be recognized as a major social problem in Europe (Hagemann-White 2001; Logar 2011).

As those who have conducted such quantitative surveys will know, these are highly complex operations. From the stage of building a questionnaire to the production of results, numerous challenges face research teams. Over time, there has been an accumulation of experience and the testing of methods to facilitate the disclosure of sensitive information relating to women's personal histories, while at the same time protecting respondents from undue distress and risk of perpetrators learning of their revelations. Support is also given to interviewers who, usually for the first time, have to utter words used in the questions designed by researchers and listen to the responses of women victims of violence in order to gather accounts that are as "true" as possible to the realities experienced by these women. It is these realities that research teams seek to reveal through the analysis of the data collected. Given the diversity of contexts and relationships in which violent acts occur, combined with the variety of social and demographic characteristics and trajectories of women, the challenge facing researchers is colossal. At every stage, words must be found to label statistical indicators, to give meanings to statistical relationships (from correlations to causal explanations), and to refer to the protagonists in violent acts.

This process of naming is grounded in scientific methodologies and in theoretical advances in understanding social phenomena. Yet, when the results are released into the public domain, the words and the meanings they are intended to convey become political objects. Their usage can then be transformed as they are spoken or written by a plethora of journalists, activists, politicians, and other social actors. They are no longer the property of the researchers who employed them in the titles of journal articles or reports, in chapter headings or in the lists of variables in statistical tables. As stressed by Pierre Bourdieu, for language to impose itself as neutral depends on a practical consensus between agents or groups whose interests are partially or totally different; thus social science must take into account that language is autonomous (Bourdieu, 1982:18–20).

We will begin by discussing the case of the French survey on violence against women (subsequently referred to as Enveff survey) and how a statistic became a "social fact" (Maillochon 2007). The issue of reception of published survey results on this politically sensitive topic will then be examined from the perspective of the messages that are heard, some of them welcomed, some ignored, others refuted or challenged, asking why this is so. Finally, we will pursue the theme of what is at stake when communicating survey results at the European level and the limitations to the building of a European "language of violence."

Statistical Indicators: A Powerful Tool for Shaping Concepts and Meanings

Over the last forty years, the European "general public" has become accustomed to receiving information containing statistics. During this period, social surveys became an integral part of the workings of society. Whether the objectives are principally to inform policy or "purely" academic, the gathering of information directly from statistically representative individuals and the publication of results in the media remain a recognized method of understanding population and societal trends, and such reporting has become a daily occurrence. Statements such as "one in five people," "one in three households," or "on average . . ." are assumed now to be understood by the receiver. This familiarity thus apparently exempts the information giver of the necessity to explain how the prevalence rate or the scale of the phenomenon being discussed has been calculated—as well as how it has been defined.

The use of statistics in association with certain words has contributed to giving new meanings to these words. This potential to create new meanings can be a positive attribute of language, expanding linguistic repertoires. However, the potential to transform may be used intentionally to shape the way others represent the world and signify and label objects and notions (Wareing 1999; Bourdieu 1982). In so doing, the aim may be to manipulate perceptions and understandings—to generate negative attitudes or even fears. The repetition of words in association gradually confirms the relationship between the objects they signify (e.g., "delinquency" linked with the notions of "lone parents" or "absent fathers"). The link is then compounded by the use of statistics, as "scientific proof" of its strength and validity.

The language of academic research, in objectifying relationships and processes, "cuts up reality" (Singh 1999) in a particular way. The challenge then is to translate from scientific jargon into generally accessible language. This is an important instance of the power of academia: the words and expressions used to convey key findings, the construction of the "scientific message," and the choice of the results to be communicated. It is our role as academic researchers in the field of gender-based violence studies that is to be examined here. How have we "cut up reality" in our analysis of violence, the design of surveys and the development of questionnaires, the fabrication of indicators, the publication of results? How have we responded to the demands of politicians or to those of the media in our communication of survey results?

In academic publications of survey results, one usually finds justifications for methodological decisions and the construction of statistical indicators. The latter are the fruit of months of arduous preparation of the survey instrument, supervising fieldwork, then intricate analyses of reported acts and their contextualization (relationship to the perpetrator, place, time, demographic characteristics, and social status of victims). A major challenge to research teams has been to find the appropriate terminology to communicate these results to politicians, social services, and other user groups, plus more generally to civil society. Violent acts had to be labeled succinctly, the context of their occurrence specified, and—with a view to informing policy—the characteristics of individuals or groups particularly "at risk" needed to be defined. Despite efforts to explain the object under study, the survey design, the categories used, and what can or cannot be explicated from results, it is rare that the use of published "rates" and "percentages" in political discourse and in the media reflects such precautions taken. These arenas are more concerned with labeling the victims—and, implicitly, the perpetrators—than enlightening the public on the processes leading to violence. Careful definitions of types and contexts of violence, located within specific time periods, are lost within general statements such as "one in ten women are victims of violence by their partner" (one of the first results of the French survey revealed to the public and, as we will discuss, related at frequent intervals on radio, television, or in the press). We will focus here on the experience of the French survey, looking at the language choices at each stage, from the development of the questionnaire to the announcement of results via the media and their reception. The fact that particular statistical results subsequently have lived a life of their own will also be discussed (Maillochon 2007).

A French Survey on Violence against Women: A Challenge for a "Nonsexist Society"

The first aim of the research team was to contribute to the international forum working to eradicate violence against women and respond to the call from the 1995 Beijing Platform. The Beijing platform, drawn up in September 1995 at the Fourth International Conference on Women, encouraged governments to take action to prevent and eliminate violence against women. This action was to include the gathering of reliable data enabling the provision of statistics relating to the prevalence of the various forms of violence against women and to encourage research into the causes, nature, severity, and consequences of such violent acts as well as an evaluation of the efficiency of preventative measures taken by public authorities.

Quantitative surveys had already taken place in some countries, some on a local scale (e.g., in London; Hanmer and Saunders 1984) and some national (the first by Statistique Canada 1993). The issue of violence specifically directed to women had been approached in various ways: as an element of family violence in the United States (Straus and Gelles 1986), as experienced by women in cohabiting couples in Switzerland (Gillioz et al. 1997) and Netherlands (Römkens 1992), or in all contexts in Finland (Heiskanen and Piispa 1998). Toward the end of the decade, the number of surveys around the world multiplied (Population Reports 1999).

While wishing to generate indicators similar to those produced from previous surveys (Canada, Finland, Switzerland, etc.), the team needed to put together a survey that would be acceptable to French decision makers, nongovernmental organizations (NGOs), and also academics. The language and concepts would have to be appropriate to the French context.

A key decision was not to refer to "male violence" as had been done in the Canadian and Finnish surveys. French society represents itself (still) as an egalitarian society in which individuals' rights are protected by the 1789 Declaration of the Rights of Man (albeit a constitution that "forgot" women as citizens). In contrast, North American and British societies are seen as fundamentally nonegalitarian, recognizing "differences"—even giving them legitimacy as such—between population groups (class, gender, ethnic minorities). A survey focusing on "male" violence against "women," identifying intrinsic differences between men and women as social groups, would have been supported by neither politicians, the media, certain NGOs, nor most academics. Referring more generally to "violence against women," the survey thereby would not only adhere to certain cultural-political precepts but also open up the problematic to women perpetrators of violence.

Another terminological decision taken was not to use the word *violence* in the questionnaire. Rather, acts and gestures were to be set in specific contexts or relationships. The reason for this choice was the knowledge that the term *violence* was used in a number of ways and that its meaning certainly varied from person to person. During the phase of constructing the questionnaire, several in-depth interviews were conducted around the word *violence*, and the diversity of expression of what constituted violence confirmed our decision.

These terminological choices impacted on subsequent events in a number of ways. In the first instance, omitting the word *male* and opening up the range of perpetrators to relatives, colleagues, neighbors, or partners who were women gave us the confidence that we had made it possible to account for most types of violence experienced by women. At the same time, it was clear from the interviews[1] that respondents understood that our main objective was to study violence generated by unequal gender relations and male dominance or control. The impact of the second choice was more problematic. Since the questionnaire did not generate ready-made indicators of the prevalence of violence, these had to be constructed post hoc. This was our aim, in order to be able to distinguish between different forms of violence. Above all, it is the task of the scientist to produce figures that to date had been absent, leaving the way open for speculation and even fantasy. No other "objective" data on the experience of interpersonal violence were available, administrative and legal sources not including information on the victims nor on their relationship to the perpetrator.

We also believed that the context or relationship in which violence takes place was an important consideration in the diversity of types and intensity. Thus violence within intimate partner relationships or in the workplace could take place over a number of months or years, include a number of different acts, and be referred to as an "ongoing situation of violence," whereas violence experienced in the street or in a nightclub, for example, could be isolated acts and involve a perpetrator that was unknown to the victim.

This of course leads us to scrutinize not only what we consider to be "violent interpersonal relations" but also what we see as "serious violence" and "less serious violence." This ranking clearly presents a challenge. The distinction appears to imply an order of priority in policy action, and different types of violence are usually classified by institutions as one or the other, seen as more or less life threatening (e.g., "grievous bodily harm" and "attempted rape," respectively). In the Enveff survey, the organization of the questionnaire by life context made it possible to identify the diversity of types of violence, different meanings of a similar type (e.g., being hit) being generated by their taking place in different contexts (e.g., being hit by someone at work or by someone in the family). Given that intimate partner violence generally combines several types of acts over a period, indicators were developed empirically to distinguish two levels: serious violence (having reported at least one act of physical or sexual violence during the previous 12 months or repeated psychological violence or verbal abuse during the period) and very serious violence (an accumulation of at least two of these different forms). Clearly, at the time of the interview the woman may have reported violence we categorized as "serious" while she may have been subjected to "very serious" violence several years beforehand, and vice versa. The distinction "serious/very serious" was used intentionally rather than "less serious/serious" in order that both types of situation be treated as intolerable. In terms of action, however, is the distinction useful? The specific nature of intimate partner violence and other types of violence in the household lies in the duration of controlling behavior over a long period, with moments of higher intensity than others. Are women more likely to report during phases of very serious violence or when what they are experiencing is less serious but when they fear that their partner is likely to become more violent toward them? While these different levels might have meaning for local service providers, including the police, *violence in the couple* (or *domestic violence* or *intimate partner violence*) is usually the overarching term used to describe an "abnormally functioning relation-ship," in which one partner controls or attempts to control the other using physical force and/or other types of violence. It is a rather blurred notion transformed into a tangible reality through measurement.

Handing Over Words and Numbers to Civil Society, Politicians, and Academia

In December 2000, the Enveff team released the first results of the survey at a press conference in presence of the then Secretary of State for Women's Rights, Nicole Pery. As Sylvia Walby has since written, there "is a tension between the specialised definitions that have developed in the VAW expert and practitioner community and definition of related phenomena used in mainstream policy and services" (Walby, 2005: 196). An effort was made to explain the survey methodology and the aim to go beyond the concept of "battered wives" and provide a clear definition of what was covered by our use of the term *"violences conjugales."* The first press articles included these explanations. The principal results retained in subsequent weeks were that "one in ten women" had been "victims of violence at the hands of their partner" during the previous year and that this type of violence was expe-rienced by women of all social classes. In 2001, the state secretary set up a campaign against violence in the couple. As time went by, the "one in ten" statistic began to live a life of its own, quoted in numerous contexts. How-ever, the details behind the definition were rapidly lost. Another impor-tant result of the survey also fell into oblivion: the estimated 48,000 rapes each year, clearly a more difficult statistic for politicians, media, and the general public to handle. Yet the readiness to announce dramatic rates of violence was apparent again after the second press conference, giving broader results from the survey. The team presented results on violence reported in public space. Totaling together insults, slaps, physical threats, sexual harassment, sexual assault, and attempted rape, a rate of 19 percent of women experiencing one or another form of violence was announced, perhaps unwisely even though it had been stressed that 13 percent of this rate was accounted for by verbal insults. However, the rate of "one in five" women experiencing violence in public space was published the next day in the press. At a time—autumn 2001—when feelings of insecurity were increasing and the media reported unrest in the French suburban housing estates, this statistic drew attention to particular groups of young men seen as violent.

Our first publications attempted to make definitions explicit, drawing attention to the different levels and forms of violence as well as to the context in which they took place (Jaspard et al 2001). However, this did not prevent a small group of academics from accusing the team of having constructed artificial indicators to fit their objective of proving that men were essentially violent and that all women were potential victims (Romito 2003)! Indeed, a particular focus for criticism was our definition of sexual harassment—being followed in the street, being confronted by an exhibitionist, being subjected to unwanted physical contact but distinguished from sexual assault—acts we considered as violence. Objections were made to our "insinuation" that "a shy young man on a Sunday afternoon" (Iacub and Le Bras 2003) who approaches a woman, touching her, should be regarded as a perpetrator of violence. Similarly, our intimate partner violence indicator, which included verbal and psychological violence (these forms counting for the greater part of the rate announced), raised questions as to our ulterior motives. We were seen as intentionally—or even naively—adopting an "Anglo Saxon" approach and including "banal" acts and gestures in violence indicators (Romito 2003).

Such contestations can be understood by considering national identity building and the imagined attributes of the nation as a community. Strong criticism of the motives and scientificity of the French survey team, through the statistical indicators they produced, are then shown to have similar origins to those faced by the Swedish survey team: words were perceived as a threat to the image of French/Swedish societies (Lundgren and Westerstrand 2007). The criticism was linked, on the one hand, to a refutation of gender relations as a structural force and, on the other, to the political crusade to resist sexuality becoming a political issue (Fassin 2003). Thus we can speak out against violence against women, and quote rates and explanations, but naming such violence in association with the words *sex* or *sexuality*, as in the polemics around the notion of date rape in the United States, provokes rebellion (Fassin, 2003; Romito 2007). Furthermore, the refusal to acknowledge the connections between sexism and sexual violence is based on the rejection of the idea of a continuum of violence. The French research team was thus accused of fusing distinct acts and producing violence indicators with no sense (Jaspard et al 2003).

Thus we find a reticence to pronounce words—to think of the object or act to which they refer: qualitative studies into sexual harassment have revealed that various terms and expressions are used to minimize the severity or avoid considering the implications of an experience, partly through feelings of guilt. Young women may refer to "an evening that finished badly" and "a story that went wrong" rather than describe what they went through (Phillips quoted in Romito 2007:65). It is therefore evident that naming acts of violence is important for women to be able to accept their experiences as such and seek help and for practitioners to respond adequately. Naming is also necessary for measurement, to show that what has happened is not rare and is unacceptable conduct and not related to women's own behavior or feelings. In the end, we can say that the message has penetrated through the wall erected against feminist research and that women increasingly acknowledge and report that "something really happened," to paraphrase Liz Kelly and Jill Radford (1990).

Communicating Rates across Europe: Sharing or Imposing Definitions?

While many aspects of survey production are framed within the international context of a call for reliable data, prevalence survey teams have necessarily responded to national concerns. Not only did the arguments of fundraisers have to be aligned with the preoccupations of, for example, health impacts or the economic cost of violence against women (VAW), but survey teams also had to be prepared to feed into civil society debates. Survey results thus had to inform national politicians—with the aim of improving policy and innovating legislation—at the same time as satisfying the demands of grassroots organizations pushing for social change. In addition, lobbying at the European level, in preparation for EU legislation, meant that national surveys were encouraged to have broader relevance beyond the national context (Hagemann-White 2001). This has led to the circulation of terms and expressions and the formatting of published results in order to correspond to the objectives of European policy action. Given the generalized use of English in European policy debate, combined with a long history of research on VAW in the United Kingdom, this state may be largely seen as holding a hegemonic position in the imposition of terminology that is specific to the UK political and legislative context. In other European states where English is the working language (Nordic countries, Netherlands), VAW research uses a shared vocabulary, gradually expanded as definitions are refined. However, in national contexts in which use of English is not widespread, or inexistent, academics and practitioners have remained disconnected from debate and violence prevention discourse, and theoretical advances have developed their own vocabulary.

The drawing up of Europe-wide policies of prevention of violence relies on cross-national comparisons of survey data, in an effort to determine best practices. The way in which concepts from one national context are adopted and named in another is constrained by language and culture (including politics; Klein 2007; CAHRV2008). This has long been a challenge in European cross-national research on racism and ethnicity, for example. More than a question of translation, obstacles to debate and comparison arise from different philosophies of integrating foreign migrants and their offspring born in the countries of immigration. This is also an important issue for cross-national comparison on violence against women, particularly in a context in which social debates on violence seen as culturally specific are not set within the understandings of violence obtained from prevalence surveys (Condon, Lesné, and Schröttle 2011).

During the Coordination Action on Human Rights Violations (CAHRV), funded through the European Commission's 6th Framework Program, we and our other colleagues working on the comparative analysis of European prevalence surveys used a pragmatic approach to arrive at terms that would describe the same types of acts or relationships (Schröttle et al. 2006). From the outset, it was necessary to be explicit about the composition of indicators used in the production of survey results. Only then could we hope to find common denominators—concepts that signified acts or experiences as similar as possible.

It is interesting to consider how some terms have become imposed in European debate and then transposed into national contexts. Very often, terms are translated literally—usually from English—into other European languages, even when the term or expression is not commonplace or may even be misunderstood.

The use of the term *domestic violence* is an example. Over the years, it has been used in policy documents and international debate as if ubiquitously understood throughout Europe, yet are we all referring to the same context of violence, the same actors? International literature has tended to use the term *domestic violence* to refer to situations of ongoing violence in married or cohabiting couples. In the French context, the term *domestique* relates to the household and, used in conjunction with *violence*, refers to more than the relationship between intimate partners. Such imprecision has not stopped non-English-speaking researchers in France or other countries from importing the term, so that expressions such as "*les violences domestiques,*" "*la violencia domestica,*" and so forth are encountered. However, strong arguments to be used in lobbying at the national level must be based on words that have a meaning for the message to be heard.

Another example is the term *stalking*. Lobbying by British feminists resulted in such violence being recognized as constituting a criminal act. It corresponds to a particular form of harassment. This is not so in France, where there is no corresponding term. Its use of course has an impact on what is covered by the notion of sexual harassment and thus on measurement of this form of violence.

Concluding Remarks

It is our duty as academics to produce new knowledge while being open about the methods used and what the words used to express this knowledge actually mean. The key role of statistics in various arenas of everyday life has been examined here through our particular involvement in communicating results of prevalence surveys on violence against women. Language, from the phrasing of survey questions to the delivering of results, or even at the stage of presenting a case for such studies to funders, will have specific impacts. We are increasingly aware that a great deal of thought must be put into how words and numbers are linked to produce the chosen message. Invited to produce sound scientific evidence based on statistics, we have no option but to "cut up reality," as well as to combine parts of this reality when underlying processes serve to form a whole: from acts to the continuum of violence.

A major challenge that has faced our quest to build a European voice is that of crossing language barriers: between disciplines, between sections of civil society, between national and regional languages. The challenge that still faces us is to ensure that communication moves in both directions, from either side of the barrier. Not only must our academic language be understood, but we also must continue to listen to the words spoken by women, be they victims, activists, or practitioners. And bridges must be built so that concepts and ways of naming and framing debate and violence prevention may benefit from the experiences outside English-language contexts. In writing this chapter, the author has discussed the notions used in the French survey. Yet this involved translating the French term *violences* into the English term *violence*. We may ponder over how the French use of the plural may be an efficient way of alluding to the plurality of forms and contexts comprising the continuum, whereas in English, the term is in the singular.

References

Bourdieu, Pierre. (1982). *Ce que parler veut dire*. Paris: Fayard. (English translation: *Language and Symbolic Power*. Cambridge: Polity Press, 1991).

CAHRV (Coordination Action on Human Rights Violations). (2008). *Gendering Human Rights Violations: The Case of Interpersonal Violence*. EU Research on Social Sciences and Humanities. http://www.cahrv.uni-osnabrueck.de/reddot/CAHRV_final_report_-_complete_version_for_WEB.pdf.

Condon, Stéphanie, and the Enveff team. (2004). "A Quantitative Approach to Understanding Violence against Women: The National Survey on Violence against Women in France." In R. Klein and B. Wallner (eds.), *Conflict, Gender and Violence*, 137–56. Vienna: StudienVerlag.

Condon, Stéphanie, Maud Lesné, and Monika Schröttle. (2011). "What Do We Know about Gendered Violence and Ethnicity across Europe from Surveys?" In Ravi Thiara, Stéphanie Condon, and Monika Schröttle, *Violence against Women and Ethnicity: Commonalities and Differences across Europe*, 59–76. Opladen: Barbara Budrich.

Fassin, Eric. (2003). *Liberté, égalité, sexualité: Actualité politique des questions sexuelles (entretiens avec Clarisse Fabre)*. Paris: Editions Belfond/Le Monde.

Gillioz, L., J. De Puy, and V. Ducret. (1997). *Domination et violence envers la femme dans le couple.* Lausanne: Editions Payot Lausanne.

Hagemann-White, Carol. (2001). "European Research on the Prevalence of Violence against Women." *Violence against Women* 7 (7):732–59.

Hanmer, J., and S. Saunders. (1984). *Well-Founded Fear:A Community Study of Violence to Women.* London: Hutchinson.

Heiskanen, M., and M. Piispa. (1998). *Faith, Hope and Battering. A Survey of Mens' Violence in Finland.* Helsinki: Statistics Finland.

Iacub, M. and H. Le Bras (2003). "Homo mulieri lupus: à propos d'une enquête sur les violences envers les femmes." *Les Temps Modernes* 623 (February-March-April): 112–34.

Jaspard, Maryse. (2005). *Les violences contre les femmes.* Paris: La Découverte, collection Repères.

Jaspard, Maryse, Elizabeth Brown, Stéphanie Condon, Jean-Marie Firdion, Dominique Fougeyrollas-Schwebel, Annick Houel, Brigitte Lhomond, Florence Maillochon, Marie-Josephe Saurel-Cubizolles, and Marie-Ange Schiltz. (2003). *Enquête nationale sur les violences envers les femmes en France.* Paris: La Documentation Française.

Jaspard, Maryse, and the Enveff team. (2001). "Violence against Women: The First French National Survey." *Population et Sociétés* 364: http://www.ined.fr/en/resources_documentation/publications/pop_soc/bdd/publication/138.

Jaspard, Maryse, and the Enveff team. (2003). "Violences vécues, fantasmes et simulacres . . ." *Les Temps Modernes* 624 (May-June-July): 184–95.

Kelly, Liz, and Jill Radford. (1990). "'Nothing Really Happened': The Invalidation of Women's Experiences of Sexual Violence." *Critical Social Policy* 10: 39–53.

Klein, Renate. (2007). "Construire une voix européenne pour exprimer les violences interpersonnelles." In Maryse Jaspard and Stéphanie Condon (eds.), *Nommer et compter les violences envers les femmes en Europe: Enjeux scientifiques et politiques,* 157–61. Paris: Institut de Démographie, Université de Paris.

Logar, Rosa. (2011). "Violence against Women: Still a Political Problem throughout Europe." In Ravi Thiara, Stéphanie Condon, and Monika Schröttle (eds.), *Violence against Women and Ethnicity: Commonalities and Differences across Europe,* 35–58. Opladen: Barbara Budrich.

Lundgren, Eva, G. Heimer, J. Westerstrand, and A.-M. Kalliokoski. (2002). *Captured Queen: Men's Violence against Women in "Equal" Sweden; A*

Prevalence Study. Umeå: Brottsoffermyndigheten and Uppsala University, Fritzes Offentliga Publikationer.

Lundgren, Eva, and Jenny Westerstrand. (2007). "Enquêtes sur les violences envers les femmes:Des contextes politiques contrasté au sein de la région nordique." In Maryse Jaspard and Stéphanie Condon (eds.), *Nommer et compter les violences envers les femmes en Europe: Enjeux scientifiques et politiques*, 49–54. Paris: Institut de Démographie, Université de Paris.

Maillochon, Florence. (2007). "'Chiffres noirs' contre 'chiffres ronds': l'Enquête Enveff dans la presse quotidienne française (2000–2004)." In Maryse Jaspard and Natacha Chetcuti (eds.), *Violences envers les femmes: "Trois pas en avant, deux pas en arrière!" Réflexions autour d'une enquête en France*, 41–58. Paris: Harmattan, La bibliothèque du féminisme.

Population Reports. (1999). "Ending Violence against Women." *Population Reports* 27 (4): 1–44.

Romito, Patrizia. (2003). "Les attaques contre les enquêtes sur les violences envers les femmes, ou qui a peur des chiffres sur les violences commises par les hommes." *Nouvelles Questions Féministes* 22 (3): 82–87.

Romito, Patrizia. (2007). "Recherches qualitatives et quantitatives dans l'étude des violences envers les femmes." In Maryse Jaspard and Natacha Chetcuti (eds.), *Violences envers les femmes: "Trois pas en avant, deux pas en arrière!" Réflexions autour d'une enquête en France*, 59–73. Paris: Harmattan, La bibliothèque du féminisme.

Römkens, R. (1992). *Gewoon geweld? Omwang, aard, gevolgen en achtergronden van geweld tegen vrouwen in heteroseksuele relaties*. Amsterdam: Svets and Zeitlinger.

Schröttle, Monika, Manuela Martinez, S. Condon, M. Jaspard, M. Piispa, J. Westerstrand, J. Reingardiene, M. Springer-Kremser, C. Hagemann-White, P. Brzank, C. May-Chahal, and B. Penhale. (2006). "Comparative Reanalysis of Prevalence of Violence against Women and Health Impact Data in Europe—Obstacles and Possible Solutions: Testing a Comparative Approach on Selected Studies." CAHRV. http://www.cahrv.uni-osnabrueck.de/reddot/190.htm.

Singh, Ishtla. (1999). "Language, Thought and Representation." In Linda Thomas et al., *Language, Society and Power: An Introduction*, 1–16. London: Routledge.

Statistique Canada. (1993). "L'enquête sur les violences envers les femmes; Survey archive." Accessed June 9, 2013. http://www23.statcan.gc .ca/imdb/p2SV_f.pl?Function=getSurvey&SDDS=3896&Item_Id =1712&lang=fr.

Straus, M. A., and R. J. Gelles. (1986). "Societal Change and Change in Family Violence from 1975 to 1985 as Revealed by Two National Surveys." *Journal of Marriage and the Family* 48: 465–79.

Walby, Sylvia. (2005). "Improving Statistics on Violence against Women." *Statistical Journal of the United Nations Economic Commission for Europe* 22 (4): 193–216.

Wareing, Shân. (1999). "What Is Language and What Does It Do?" In Linda Thomas et al., *Language, Society and Power: An Introduction*, 17–34. London: Routledge.

Note

1. A member of the research team was present during most of the telephone interview sessions.

4

"Clouds Darkening the Blue Marital Sky"

How Language in Police Reports (Re)Constructs Intimate Partner Homicides

Daniela Gloor and Hanna Meier, Switzerland

Introduction

This chapter examines language and textual practices of police investigation files on homicides in intimate relationships. The analyses draw
on so called final police reports, which, in the criminal justice system of
several Swiss Cantons, constitute the key document in the crime investigation process and serve as a crucial basis for prosecution, judgment,
and sentencing.[1] In these final reports, police investigators summarize all
facts and facets of the homicide that they consider relevant and thus give
an account of what happened during the homicide and what led up to
it. Their task, as stated in the code of criminal procedure, is to "investigate material truth."[2] It is in the document of the final police report that
a homicide is institutionally defined for the first time and becomes substantially shaped as a specific case. Although there is an extensive literature
on homicide research—mainly originating in North America, less so in
Europe—studies with an institutional focus, especially on the interpreta-
tive performances of police investigators, are rare.[3]

Underlying our empirical research is the presumption that homicides—as
indictable incidents that are publicly investigated and represented in written record—have to be understood as products of linguistic and textual

processes. This means that not only reconstruction of what happened ("material truth") but to a large extent also construction of what happened is significant to this work, and these processes are to be analyzed.

We first explain the theoretical frame we are using for our qualitative analyses of written documents and present a textual model that will guide our approach to the police reports. We then describe the empirical data: records of intimate partner homicides—that is, mainly femicides. Our presentation of the findings then focuses on "denominating strategies": the specific terms used in the reports to refer to the actual homicide. We scrutinize the ways in which events prior to the homicide such as previous history and background are described in the reports. The chapter ends with conclusions about relevant characteristics of language use and terminology in police homicide reports and inquires after the effects of the specific wording.

Theoretical Frame

Police Files as Textual Documents

In the final report, the police furnish all information and consideration regarding the incident they have acquired during the investigation. More precisely, what is assembled in the account—and shaped into a "story"—is the information that is considered relevant and worth communicating to the reader so as to establish coherence and confirmable comprehensibility of what happened. Schönert describes this procedure as a "stylising process of story telling": "In the practice of penal enquiry and interrogation the many possible stories to an incident are cut down to a chosen few stories that are to be combined into one fact abiding, consistent story—the 'facts of the case' or 'circumstances'—adapted for judgment" (Schönert 1991b: 14; translated by the authors). Institutional requirements and regulations on how to draw up such documents are, as we find, vague. There are no specific instructions or guidelines for writing homicide reports; instead, the common report guidelines are applied.[4]

From a methodological point of view the examined documents are "natural," "nonstandardized" data (Soeffner 1989a). We prefer the more accurate term of "process produced data" (Eisner 1997). Process-produced data consist in material products—mainly textual documents that are created, in one way or another, through institutional (often state) activities. Thus these data originate from specific contexts of institutional practices that are completely detached from the research process. It is exactly this aspect that makes police records very valuable when it comes to the examination of language use and linguistic processes and their meaning in regard to problem definition and perception.

Penal procedures constitute—right from the beginning of police assessment and investigation up to the conclusive court proceedings—sites of a collective construction of social reality (Löschper 1999; Soeffner 1989b; *gesellschaftliche Konstruktion sozialer Wirklichkeit*). Ulrike Gleixner (1995) describes documents produced by institutional agents in the course of penal procedures as "*Wahrheitstexte*" ("texts of truth"). These texts (have to) display specific qualities and attributes that make them "utilisable" for those procedures.[5] Scholars in social research and the history of literature increasingly conceive of such texts as a unique literary category and examine their particular formal and textual features.[6] According to Wolfgang Naucke (1991) as well as Ludger Hoffmann (1991) such texts feature distinct stylistic figures that turn debatable events into "legally relevant circumstances" (*Sachverhalt*). Three figures of textual stylizing matter in particular:

1. Textual stylizing of the circumstances happens by "reducing the amount of facts" to professional necessities—as defined by law (Naucke 1991). In other words, the documents primarily discuss what is of interest and wanted from a judicial or a legal point of view (Gleixner 1995). In the course of penal procedures the complexity and the abundance of information progressively—with each step of putting things down in writing—are reduced to those elements of action and such elements of interpretation that are of penologic concern. It starts with recording interrogations that mold oral statements into written form—a documentation process that filters and weights the interview situation into a concise protocol, phrased by the police, not the interrogated. The writing of the final police report presents a next step of filtering and emphasizing information and thus establishes the "circumstances." Setting up the bill of indictment and eventually putting forward the verdict take this process of reduction and construction still further. Out of the vast amount of details, gradually those are distilled that matter judicially and constitute a specific offense: "murder with malicious intent," "culpable homicide," "manslaughter," "grievous bodily harm," "assault," and so on. Content and language of the texts are (progressively) shaped by legal norms.

2. A second stylizing figure in text production is the construction of facts "fit for truth" ("*wahrheitsfähige*" *Fakten*; Naucke 1991). The textual task consists in conveying verifiable and reliable knowledge— that is, in presenting findings as "true"—for the (future) court verdict has to be based on facts and truth.[7] The term "facts fit for truth" already indicates a fundamental challenge inherent to reconstruction: past reality—as it really has happened—is never fully nor in complete certainty reconstructable.[8] Accordingly, in the (re)construction of facts the mode of description shifts from "truth" to "plausibility," as Hoffmann (1991) shows: "Fit for truth" becomes that which can be presented as plausible. To manufacture plausibility, textual construction uses three strategies:

   • "Normalizing": events are evaluated against the criterion of everyday logic and are described in reference to this criterion;
   • Answering "expectations of coherence": details have to be brought into an agreeable sequence that becomes "verifiable" by comparisons, connections, and repetitions; and
   • "Personalizing": delivered information is linked to the credibility of its sources (Hoffmann 1991: 89ff.).

   A very effective way to achieve a text production of "facts fit for truth" is the use of the narrative form: "Truth" essentially is grounded in a "good" (i.e., plausible) story.[9] "Progressive story construction constitutes the background against which causes of action are introduced and assessed" (Hoffmann 1991: 91; translated by the authors).

3. The third stylizing figure concerns the "form-bound" making (*Formgebundenheit*) of the texts (Naucke 1991). Penal procedures and corresponding documents do not allow for free descriptions or free accounts of the circumstances. Rather, procedural, formal demands (code of criminal procedure, penal law) as well as institutional processes and customary practices form the notation type of particular documents such as records, final reports, bills of indictment, and verdicts.

Though reality (re)constructed in homicide files always is to be understood as professionally and institutionally shaped (stylized) reality, this implies by no means that these texts are free from nonprofessional, everyday interpretation patterns. To the contrary, "juridical recordings of

"criminal" events—in particular those of lower authorities—also comprise
notions and description patterns coming from everyday and literary discourse on criminality" (Schönert 1991b: 17; translated by the authors). It
is important to note that this holds true as well for "superior authorities."[10]
Everyday knowledge and concepts are present in the texts as well as collectively shared and therefore generally intelligible interpretation patterns.[11]
Those patterns function as "superordinate schemata" (*vorgeordnete Schemata*; Sauer 1989) that enhance the plausibility of the (re)construction of
circumstances.[12] It becomes obvious that the persuasive power and the "fit-
ness for truth" of an account of the circumstances is not only determined
by professional logic and institutionally prescribed structuring of the narrated facts. The narration of what happened is also—as a further text layer
(*Textschicht*)[13]—"structured by social discourses and notions of regulation
as well as informal norms and patterns of perception and interpretation"
of the debated situations—that is, the recorded events (Töngi 2004: 21;
translated by the authors). The explicit or implicit reference to everyday
knowledge and interpretation patterns ascertains—apart from penologic
considerations—a common meaningful basis that writer and reader share.
It is this frame of reference that supports the acceptability of the account
as plausible—and thus as true. Therefore, as regards language, final police
reports draw on professional juridical terminology and stylization as well
as on everyday stocks of linguistic figures and concepts.

These processes of text production make police files particularly interesting data to analyze: "Texts document what participants [i.e., the "objects"
of research] are actually doing in the world" (Silverman 2006: 157). Thus
we see the social production and shaping of police documents not as a
handicap, in the sense that the validity of the "represented" may be limited, but rather as an asset and topic for research. In other words, thorough
analyses of textual strategies and language used in the reports prove a very
valuable method to examine the patterns of relevance and lines of reasoning of the police; these emerge in the specific wording.

Textual Model

The following model gives insight into the formal features and structuring
of the documents, their text types, and their segments. It is to be read as
an analytical tool, since reports do not show distinct separation between

different kinds of information and text types or mark the transition from one type of information to another.

We distinguish two discrete types of information (*Informationsebenen*) in the documents that basically fulfill different functions and also differ as text types. The first concerns police actions and procedures in connection with the homicide. The second concerns the actual incident under consideration and the outcome and conclusions of the investigation.

Information about Police Actions and Procedures
Detailed information about police proceedings (from the first notification of an incident up to the completion of investigations) represents a substantial part of the files. This self-referential information, rather than being contained in designed sequences, is spread out through the entire document. Such passages answer an implicit self-questioning of the police: What did we do exactly? Did our actions conform to protocol? Were they executed correctly? Concerning style and text type, the passages on police actions display a pronounced documenting and legitimizing character.[14] (See Table 4.1.) Recurrent and detailed declaration of dates, locations, names and ranks, and so on underscore this legitimizing style. The aim is to prove that the actions and measures taken were correct according to law and police directives. By explicitly demonstrating that police proceed impeccably according to professional standards, these text passages link tightly with the second, content-related information: Ever-present in the report and interlinked with information about the incident, they contribute to the construction of objectivity and truthfulness of the account.

Table 4.1 Text model for final police reports

Text relates to . . .		Type of questions (aim)	Text form and purpose
. . . police actions (1)	Investigation procedure, measures	What did we do? Is it correct?	documenting, legitimizing
. . . the offense (2)	Happenings before, during, and after the deed	What? Who? How?	descriptive, narrating, concrete, specific
	Motive and background of the deed	Why?	interpretative, substantiating, giving reasons, constructing sense, establishing context, conceptual

Information about the Incident and Results of the Investigation
This second content-related type of information involves numerous specifications about the offense and the insights police gathered during the investigation. The text sequences with this information meet the reader's expectation to be offered all relevant aspects of the homicide. Their function is to give a concise and comprehensive description of what happened—that is, to (re)construct the circumstances. In doing so these text passages give answers to two different sets of questions: "What, Who, and How?" and "Why?"

The first set of questions concerns the concrete specifics of the case from a police point of view. *What* has happened—what kind of offense: theft, robbery, accomplished or attempted homicide? *Who* is involved in the incident—who figures as perpetrator(s) and as victim(s), and which additional persons ought to be considered? *How* did the incident pass—what was the sequence of events before, during, and after the incident? What actions were performed by whom? Concerning style and text type, the passages relating to (implicit) "What, Who, and How?" questions mainly have narrative form, including descriptions, illustrative depictions, and the (re)telling of accounts of various informants. It is in these sequences that the actual story, the specific circumstances, is vividly reconstructed with the help of evidence and findings from police interrogation.

The second question concerns the "Why?" Why did the homicide occur? Which knowledge or background information may explain it? What are the circumstances and context that have to be considered as relevant? Which motives emerged or can be suggested? Text passages dealing with the "Why?" construct significant circumstances and context around what happened. These sequences interpret and weight the information on the "What, Who, and How?" and use investigatory knowledge to construct a meaningful progress of events. Concerning style and text type, these passages show an argumentative character. Substantiating text sequences not only deliver specific reasons and explanations for the case but also corroborate the coherency and plausibility of the furnished narration concerning the reconstructed sequence of events.

The analytical distinction between these different textual features and functions in the reports provides an initial framework for analyzing the police reports and helps break them up for deeper analyses.

Empirical Basis

The data for our analysis come from the final police reports of all cases prosecuted as attempted or completed homicides in the context of intimate or family relationships that occurred in the Swiss Canton Aargau over a period of ten years (1995–2004). These were cases in which the offender and the victim were or had been in some type of close relationship or where a close relationship constituted a decisive context for the offense. This included intimate partner homicides as well as cases in which a sexual rival was the victim and cases in which a member of the nuclear or extended family was victim.

During 1995–2004 the Canton Aargau prosecuted a total of 38 attempted or completed homicides. In 15 cases the victim was killed; 23 cases were attempted homicides. For both types of offense, completed and attempted, most cases—2 out of 3—concerned intimate relationships: 10 out of 15 completed homicides were intimate homicides (67 percent); 5 cases concerned the homicide of a family member or relative (33 percent). Among the attempted homicides, 16 out of 23 cases were intimate homicides (70 percent) and 7 cases concerned a family member or relative (30 percent). Regarding gender, the analyzed cases divide as follows: Across all 26 intimate homicide cases (attempted and completed) 24 offenders (92 percent) were male and 2 offenders were female (8 percent). Of the victims, 18 were female (69 percent) and 8 were male (31 percent). Across the 12 homicide cases against family members and relatives (completed and attempted), 9 offenders (75 percent) were male and 3 offenders were female (25 percent). The victims were in 5 cases male (42 percent), in 4 cases female (33 percent), and in 3 cases small children below six years (25 percent).

The findings presented in this chapter refer mostly to police files of completed homicides. The final police reports for these cases turned out to be much more extensive and elaborated—and thus more profitable for text analyses—than those for attempted homicides.[15] Investigations on accomplished homicides are significantly more time consuming and the number of interrogations is markedly higher; they are executed by expert professionals in comparison to all-around police staff in the case of attempted homicides.[16]

Results

Naming the Deed

Throughout the report police writers very often and in different circumstances have to refer to the actual incident—that is, the act of the killing. In other words, by writing down what happened they need to address the occurrences and make use of expressions that name the action. In regards to language use and its power to shape meaning and perception, a straightforward approach consists in analyzing the wording chosen to denominate the deed. At first sight the situation might seem quite obvious. The files are dealing with completed homicides; we thus may expect that terminology reflects this fact by naming the deed as homicide. Yet, there is more variety to be found in the texts.

In order to examine terminology and its consequences, we used a subsample of six reports for which we systematically gathered every single expression that referred to the act of the homicide. The sampled reports cover two intimate homicides in current relationships as well as two in ex-relationships and two homicides between family members/relatives. For these cases we assembled a broad range of designations used. Analysis of these terms allows sorting them according to language qualities and connotations. In doing so, four categories of terms can be distinguished, and each goes along with different implications of the wording:

- Neutral dimension: *deed, act, action*
- Factual dimension: *killing, kill*
- Penal dimension: *homicide, homicide offense, offense*
- Moral dimension: *crime, murder*[17]

Whereas for instance "the act" or "the deed" remains neutral and undetermined, "the killing" states the factual situation. Specifying the killing as "homicide" or "homicide offense" (*Tötungsdelikt; Straftat*) brings the penal aspect to the foreground. Using terms such as "the murder" again implies another dimension—the one of moral assessment.

Obviously the task of reporting implies the necessity to use some kind of terminology for naming the action that is under consideration, yet at the same time the chosen wording conveys further meaning. Examination of the reports reveals systematic differences in regard to the presence of the various terms. We find a link between the type of the perpetrator-victim relationship and the naming practice (see Table 4.2). Specifically, the more intimate a relationship is, the more often terms are present in the reports that represent the neutral or factual dimension. On the other hand, in reports about homicides between family members, terms are more frequent that emphasize the seriousness of the act by invoking its penal or moral dimension.

In cases of intimate homicides, the writers of the police reports are less inclined to use words that explicitly connote the penologic implications or moral dimensions of the action. This is even more accentuated when the homicide is committed in a current relationship compared to a former relationship. In comparison to the words used to report on the killing of family members or relatives, we may interpret displayed language use when an intimate partner (mostly a woman) is killed as a strategy of normalization or trivialization. Since referral to the actual act of the killing, the homicide, is present throughout the whole document of police reports, the respective wording accompanies the entire account and thus subtly permeates the reader's perception of the reported incidents: Homicides of the (ex)woman partner aren't to be perceived as serious crimes, whereas homicides in the context of family or relatives are to be seen as severe crimes.

Reporting on Relationships and Violence

Let's turn to the reports dealing with intimate (ex)partner homicides—by far the biggest group of documents we have examined. Except for one case, these completed homicides all involve male perpetrators. Only one document deals with a case in which the wife killed her husband; all others concern homicides of (ex)wives or (ex)partners by their male (ex)partner,

Table 4.2   Naming the deed in police homicide reports

Wording and connotated dimensions		Intimate relationship (2 cases)	Ex-intimate relationship (2 cases)	Family members (2 cases)
Neutral/ factual	"Deed," "act" "Killing"	78%	49%	30%
Penal/ moral	"Homicide offense" "Crime," "murder"	22%	51%	70%
	Number of terms used	N = 49	N = 59	N = 91

and in one case the husband killed a man whom he saw as a sexual rival. A review of these reports reveals the remarkable finding that the question of previous violence against the woman (victim of the homicide) is not addressed at all in any of these documents. Domestic violence does not become a topic of discussion in the texts, which, from an investigatory point of view, are supposed to reconstruct all (possibly) relevant facts and circumstances of the homicide. In not a single report did police establish a connection between preceding violent behavior against the victim and the actual lethal offense. This finding is remarkable in light of the empirically well-documented fact that intimate partner homicides frequently have a history of prior violence—in most cases against the eventual victim—and that nonlethal domestic violence is a risk factor for lethal domestic violence.[18]

However, despite the fact that final reports do not discuss or document any prior histories of domestic violence, practically all the reports nevertheless contain implicit references to such histories, as we will show. Thus we may speak of a concurrent presence and absence of domestic violence in the reports. What is the meaning or purpose of such incongruity? And how does it occur? These findings and questions lead us to the very heart of textual constructions and the power of wording to frame understandings of criminal acts.

As we have demonstrated with our model, police reports comprise diverse textual layers and text or information types. They display characteristic ways of construction with textual interactions between what we call "concretes" ("specifics") and "concepts." A lot of specific, detailed information and particulars are recorded and compiled; this information constitutes the basis for (re)constructing the case and cause of events. It is of a highly tangible nature and provides illustrative material, which we refer to as "concretes" ("specifics"). The presentation of concretes is accompanied by another type of text with very different features: summarizing, general statements. Such passages consist of abstract statements that condense investigatory knowledge into what we call "concepts": statements that reflect interpretation-performance and meaning-construction, or similar efforts to conceive and conceptualize what happened. In the police reports, text passages with "concretes" ("specifics") and "concepts" alternate and merge consistently, and thus reinforce each other.[19]

Regarding our initial question about documenting prior domestic violence and the finding that such violence is at once present and absent from the reports, we now may clarify: In the "concretes" ("specifics"), violent incidents and behavior are present. In contrast, in "concepts," these factual bits of information are not conceptualized as domestic violence. On the level of interpretation and sense making, domestic violence is absent. Instead of understanding the available, concrete investigatory evidence of prior violence as actual violence—as domestic violence—the reports interpret such specifics in terms of other concepts, in particular the notion of "bad relationship." The notion of "bad relationship" is granted strong explanatory power and is repeatedly constructed as the context for "understanding" the homicide.[20]

In the following we show characteristics of language and phrasing that frame police reporting on relationship and violence. The effect of specific language use and related interpretation patterns is the "disappearance" of prior domestic violence from the homicide. This means no less than that a significant context of intimate homicides is neither considered nor reported even if there is explicit evidence of a prior history of domestic violence.

Actorless Presentation of (Bad) Relationships

Text sequences that describe the relationship between perpetrator and victim display—in the case of intimate partners—a typical way of representation: the actual persons in the relationship hardly ever show up in the reports. Relationships are described as though they were a "conglomerate" of blended entities rather than a context in which discernible, individual persons relate to one another by acting in specific ways.[21] Thus the phrasing used in the reports does not reveal actors but presents the relationship as though it possessed an agency of its own. Examples of wording in which this happens include alleging abstract processes and a frequent use of impersonal pronouns: "there were quarrels . . . ," "married life worsened . . . ," "the relationship darkened . . . ," "it happened . . ." The effect of such wording is that the relationship appears as responsible for what is going on rather than the people in the relationship. A further consequence of actorless accounts of relationships as conglomerates consists in constructing a common overall situation that implies substantial commonality and mutuality between the two partners. The following citation gives insight into such actorless presentation:

Due to increasingly frequent verbal disagreements the situation in the marriage of [family name] was worsening in recent years. Because the couple [family name] had considerably different moral values concerning financial investments, renovation of the house, leisure activities, clothing and vacations, repeated quarrels about these topics ensued. (Report 12, Par. 354)

[Original: Durch immer häufigere verbale Auseinandersetzungen spitzte sich die Situation in der Ehe [Familienname] in den vergangenen Jahren zu. Da das Ehepaar [Familienname] eine sehr unterschiedliche Wertvorstellung in Bezug auf Investition von Geld, Hausumbau, Freizeitbeschäftigung, Bekleidung und Ferien hatte, kam es wegen der gleichen Themen wiederholt zu Streitigkeiten. (*Bericht 12, Abs. 354*)]

Emphasis of reporting lays on the message that the relationship as such was "bad" or that "it" had grown bad. Individual behavior and attitudes of the partners involved—as factors that determine the situation—appear to have little importance. From the investigatory point of view, a reference to the concept of a bad relationship seems to suffice. The nature of the relationship as a quasi-autonomous determinant of events is taken for a meaningful enough context for the homicide. The declaration of a "troubled relationship" (the title of the motive section in report 8 following) appears to provide sufficient justification to serve as the motive for the homicide.

Most of the reports open the section on the actual act of killing with a paragraph entitled "background" before the report writer goes into details about the exact course of action before and during the offense, and it is in this paragraph that the "bad relationship" (once more) is outlined in a condensed form. These sequences establish the bad relationship as a significant circumstance and concept to have in mind when reading about the exact execution of the homicide (see report 11). Again, grammatical phrasing of these text passages features depersonalizing passive voice and nominalizations by which the relationship itself becomes the active subject and the role and actions of the perpetrator remain obscure. Two examples of such opening paragraphs:

8.3 Troubled relationship with [surname first name; female victim]

Concerning the relation to [surname first name; female victim] the accused was interrogated thoroughly. From the 21 pages of the specific interrogation record follows clearly that the relationship was not harmonious in any way. Altercations and separations alternated in regular intervals with reconciliations. Apparently there were numerous reasons for the mutual attacks, not only because of [first name; male perpetrator's son]. Yet it is to assert that both parties mutually and repeatedly sought contact and responded again respectively after differences and separations. (Report 8, Par. 947–48)

6.1. Background

The personal situation and the ugly circumstances, which ruled among [surname first name; male perpetrator] and [surname maiden name first name; female victim] since several years, and which are proved according to own statements as well as statements of many third parties, have been dealt with on various occasions. (Report 11, Par. 702–3)

[Original: 8.3. Bewegtes Verhältnis zu [Name Vorname; weibliches Opfer]

Bezüglich des Verhältnisses zu [Name Vorname; weibliches Opfer]wurde der Beschuldigte eingehend einvernommen. Aus dem 21-seitigen spezifischen Abhörungsprotokoll geht eindeutig hervor, dass das Verhältnis in keiner Art und Weise harmonisch verlief. Auseinandersetzungen und Trennungen lösten sich mit Versöhnungen in regelmässigen Abständen ab. Gründe für die gegenseitigen Attacken gab es offensichtlich viele und nicht nur wegen [Vorname; Sohn der Tatperson]. Es kann aber festgestellt werden, dass beide Parteien nach Differenzen und Trennungen den Kontakt zueinander gegenseitig immer wieder suchten, bzw.erwiderten. (Bericht 8, Par. 947–48)

Original: 6.1. Vorgeschichte

Auf die persönlichen Verhältnisse und die widrigen Umstände, welche seit mehreren Jahren zwischen [Name Vorname; männliche Tatperson] und [Name lediger Name Vorname; weibliches Opfer] geherrscht hatten und gemäss den eigenen Angaben, sowie Aussagen von zahlreichen Drittpersonen auch belegt sind, wurde verschiedentlich eingetreten. (Bericht 11, Abs. 702–3)]

Reporting on the relationship between perpetrator and victim is characterized by discharging the actors involved from their actions. Instead, a conglomerative bad relationship is described for which the issues of who took which part and who did what in "quarrels," "disputes," "attacks," or "adverse circumstances" is left hazy. This language opens a wide field of imagination that a reader may activate. The wording suggests an interpretation of mutual activity, true to the motto "it takes two to tango." Furthermore, wording manufactures the (bad) relationship as an agent of its own—to which partners somehow are exposed. And it is this "autonomously active" relationship that police reports construct as the explanatory context of the homicide. Such language use and phrasing in the reports point to inappropriate interpretation patterns concerning domestic violence and have potentially far-reaching consequences: If it is the climatic-atmospheric factor "bad relationship" that is interpreted as the relevant context of the homicide rather than individual actions, intentions, and prior violent behavior, the accountability of the perpetrator is reduced. The "bad relationship" thus appears as unfavorable circumstances and may become an exculpatory factor.

Vague Descriptions of Violent Incidents and Actions

Documenting prior violence is, as we have mentioned, not a main objective of the reports. Nevertheless, hints of physical or psychological violence as well as threats and controlling behavior are present. In cases of intimate partnership, this information is often used to exemplify the concept of a bad relationship. We have come across such an example already in the quotation from report 8, where "mutual attacks" confirm a "troubled relationship." Elsewhere the same report states that the couple canceled initiated formal proceedings for marriage "after assaults."

In regards to wording, sequences relating to prior violent incidents and behavior in intimate partnerships employ a rather vague and generic language. Incidents or comportment are not documented in detail but mentioned in a summary way, mostly using everyday speech. The wording used to describe violent actions is hardly informed by penal law. The fact that the actor of the violent acts (the perpetrator) very often is not named affirms the juridical irrelevance of prior violence, at least from the investigation's point of view. This is in contrast to the detailed documentation provided in one of the reports on a (further) assault that the perpetrator committed in custody against a warden. In that case, precise information is given on how the perpetrator acted and what exactly he did do with which effects on the victim's side (Report 37). However, documentation of prior violent behavior of the same perpetrator against his wife, the victim of the homicide, again is framed in a much less decisive way, as the following two examples demonstrate (in particular the second example from Report 37):

> That matters among husband and wife [surname, maiden name] presumably again and again became rowdy and presumably also a little rough is on the one hand proven by the statements of certain informants and on the other hand also by the broken apartment door ascertained by the police on occasion of the search from 07.11.1999. (Report 41, Par. 368)

> After his return the defendant was under the impression that his wife had changed and he assumed that meanwhile she was having a fling with

[surname first name; male person]. Because of these suspicions quarrels occurred repeatedly within the married couple, where [surname first name, male perpetrator] hit his wife in one case for certain. (Report 37, Par. 924)

[Original: Dass es zwischen den Eheleuten [Name, lediger Name] vermutlich immer wieder laut und vermutlich auch etwas grob zu-und herging, belegen einerseits die Angaben gewisser Auskunftspersonen, andererseits aber auch die anlässlich der Wohnungsdurchsuchung vom 07.11.1999 polizeilich festgestellte, aufgebrochene Wohnungstüre. (*Bericht 41, Abs. 368*)

Original: Nach der Rückkehr hatte der Beschuldigte den Eindruck, dass sich seine Frau verändert hatte und er vermutete, dass sie zwischenzeitlich ein Verhältnis mit [Name Vorname; männliche Person] hatte. Zwischen den Eheleuten kam es wegen den Verdächtigungen mehrfach zu Auseinandersetzungen, wobei [Name Vorname; männliche Tatperson] seine Ehefrau sicher einmal schlug. (*Bericht 37, Abs. 924*)]

A further characteristic feature of sequences dealing with prior abuse is that detailed, factual information about the frequency and intensity of such acts is not considered noteworthy. The same holds true for tangible effects of the violence; reports rarely mention consequences for the victim. And if the reports do so, rather slangy, everyday expressions dominate the descriptions of effects. In the following example it is the son who killed his father; the police report that it "has not been infrequent" that the father hit the mother, and concerning the effects the wording is "every now and again a black eye or other kinds of sores."

Within his family, he [victim] is said to have been the absolute boss, never allowing any "ifs and buts." Thus it wasn't a rare fact that he beat her in front of the children because of altercations or other incidents, which he did not approve of. The children had also been subjected mercilessly and had to suffer all kinds of beatings. [. . .] Thus Mrs. [surname; wife] inter alia has been noticed every now and again with a black eye or other kinds of sores. (Report 22, Par. 332, 398)[22]

[Original: Innerhalb der Familie sei er [das Opfer] der absolute Chef gewesen, ohne "Wenn und Aber" zugelassen zu haben. So sei es keine Seltenheit gewesen, dass er auch sie vor den Kindern wegen Meinungsverschiedenheiten oder anderweitigen Begebenheiten, die ihm nicht gepasst hätten, geschlagen habe. Auch die Kinder hätten sich ihm gnadenlos unterwerfen und Schläge aller Art einstecken müssen. [. . .] So wurde u.a. bei Frau [Name; Ehefrau des Opfers] hie und da ein blaues Auge oder sonstige Blessuren festgestellt. (*Bericht 22, Abs. 332, 398*)]

Concrete investigation knowledge used to prove "a bad relationship" thus may clearly indicate prior domestic violence (and—for an informed reader in this subject matter—implicitly even reveal well-known effects on the victim's side). Nevertheless, the wording of these sequences keeps the prior history vague and does not document actual, prior violence against the later victim. Nor do terminology and explanatory passages suggest any link between prior violence and the subsequent homicide under investigation—even in the case of threats to kill, as the following example shows:

For there is on the record:

- that [surname maiden name first name; female victim] lived so to speak in a state of constant distress and the chronic marriage problems burdened her emotionally deeply (register 6.14);
- that in 1987 [surname maiden name first name; female victim] apparently tried to commit suicide by taking pills (register 6.14);
- that [surname maiden name first name; female victim] took legal advice from lawyer Moor Hugo, [postcode municipality], Zelgstrasse 17, on 03.07.1995 in the matter of marital separation, independent flat, etc. (register 7.2.1); [...]
- that in the year 1996 [surname name first name; male perpetrator] threatened to kill his wife and himself, if she would separate from him, and he explained that he would agree to a divorce, but not to a marital separation (register 6.14). (Report 38, Par. 375–91)

[Original: Aktenkundig ist nämlich:

- dass [Name lediger Name Vorname; weibliches Opfer] gewissermassen in einem Dauerstress lebte und ihr die chronische Eheproblematik seelisch schwer zu schaffen machte (Register 6.14);
- dass [Name lediger Name Vorname; weibliches Opfer] im Jahre 1987 offenbar mit Tabletten aus dem Leben zu scheiden versuchte (Register 6.14);
- dass sich [Name lediger Name Vorname; weibliches Opfer] am 03.07.1995 durch Moor Hugo, lic. iur. Fürsprecher, [PLZ Gemeindename], Zelgstrasse 17, in Sachen Trennung, separate Wohnung, etc., beraten liess (Register 7.2.1); [...]
- dass [Name Vorname; männliche Tatperson] im Jahre 1996 damit drohte, seine Ehefrau und sich umzubringen, falls sich diese von ihm trennen sollte, und ausführte, dass er mit einer Scheidung einverstanden wäre, mit einer Trennung aber nicht (Register 6.14). (*Bericht 38, Abs. 375–91*)]

By means of textual analysis, we can demonstrate that final police reports do not frame previous violence as a potential context of intimate homicides. Nor does the wording used to report on prior incidents suggest that actual assaults and indictable behavior would be under discussion. We may describe the effect of language use as follows: The use of vague descriptions and everyday expressions dissociate prior violence from the reported homicide, which, in contrast, is described in a detailed, meticulous manner exploring the exact course and intent of actions, and demonstrating concrete effects. Descriptions of the homicide and the language adopted here include juridical and penal terminology. Prior domestic violence is not at all presented in this way. The obvious contrast between describing the homicide and describing prior violence and the dominant use of everyday language result in what we see as a "normalization" and "decriminalization" of previous violence against the intimate partner. The linguistic framing of prior incidents of violence thus avoids making a connection between a violent history and the homicide.

Relationships and Violence Wrapped in Metaphors

Examining the accounts of the relationship between offender and victim, we can discern another particular aspect of language use. As mentioned before, in cases of intimate homicides police commonly use the concept of "a bad relationship." To establish this concept, reports frequently make reference to a deterioration of the relationship over time: from a presumed "normal" situation the relationship takes a negative turn. Text sequences describing this process very often draw on metaphors.

Police writers recurringly use the notion of honeymoon as starting point: "harmony" or "harmonious relations" suffer from emerging "turbidity" and turn into "clouded relation." This terminology organizes a dichotomous pattern of relationship—beginning from a good situation ending in a bad one, culminating in the homicide. Contrasting "harmony" with the image of a "clouded relation" avoids further elaboration. The familiar image opens space for the reader to fill in what may constitute such clouding. The actual factors causing the "turbidity" or "misted" conditions no longer need to be explained. Use of the image implies that "we all know" what a "clouded relation" can look like. Without delivering contents and facts, the image supplies fake understanding by relying on the reader's activity. Concrete situations do not have to be documented.

After the first, apparently harmonious marital years, the marriage of [first name; male victim] and [surname name first name; female perpetrator] was clouding during the past years due to more and more frequent quarrels. (Report 12, Par. 185)

To the outside married life gave a harmonious, unimpaired impression. Quarrels and altercations within the family did not attract attention. [. . .] According to his descriptions notably the siblings [fist name; brother] and [first name; brother] had cognizance of the fact that his relationship to the wife became partly turbid. (Report 37, Par. 758)

[Original: Nach ersten, offensichtlich harmonischen Ehejahren, wurde die Ehe von [Vorname; männliches Opfer] und [Name Vorname; weibliche Tatperson] in den letzten Jahren durch immer häufigere Streitigkeiten getrübt. (Bericht 12, Abs. 185)

Original: Gegen aussen hinterliess das Eheleben einen harmonischen, intakten Eindruck. Streitigkeiten und Auseinandersetzungen in der Familie fielen nicht auf. [. . .] Seinen Schilderungen gemäss hatten namentlich die Geschwister [Vorname; Bruder] und [Vorname; Bruder] davon Kenntnis, dass sein Verhältnis zur Ehefrau teilweise getrübt war. (*Bericht 37, Abs. 758*)]

Metaphoric presentation of the relationship quite often resorts to the weather and to climate images. It is the deterioration of the relationship that these metaphors vividly speak of. Without having to go into details such as naming prior violent behavior, the metaphors suggest a decline of the relationship in the manner of changing weather patterns.[23] A "blue marital sky" becomes "overcast," "thunderclouds cover" the relationship, "weather vanes indicate storm," and there are "turmoils" to be detected in the "marital sky." The use of these images evokes an immediate and implicit "understanding" on the reader's side—tacit approval can be counted on.[24]

When exactly the first thunder clouds arose at the firstly deep blue marital sky of [surname name first name; male perpetrator] and [surname maiden name first name; female victim], couldn't, as previously mentioned several times, be dated exactly. According to the documents that are at our hands it is yet clear, that for certain the weather vanes turned to storm for a first time not only in 1997, but already in 1995 respectively supposedly even already in 1981. (Report 38, Par. 375)

Turbulences in the marital sky of [surname name first name; male perpetrator] and [surname maiden name first name; wife of perpetrator], however,

were to be registered already before her fateful acquaintance with [surname
name first name; male victim (rival)]. (Report 41, Par. 367)

[Original: Wann genau nun aber die ersten Gewitterwolken am zunächst
tiefblauen Ehehimmel von [Name Vorname; männliche Tatperson] und
[Name lediger Name Vorname; weibliches Opfer] aufgezogen sind, liess sich,
wie bereits mehrfach erwähnt, nicht genau ermitteln. Auf Grund der uns
vorliegenden Unterlagen steht jedoch fest, dass die Wetterfahnen mit Sicher-
heit nicht erst im Jahre 1997 ein erstes Mal auf Sturm gestanden sind, son-
dern bereits 1995 bzw. vermutlich sogar bereits 1981. (Bericht 38, Abs. 375)

Original: Turbulenzen am Ehehimmel von [Name Vorname; männliche Tat-
person] und [Name lediger Name Vorname; Ehefrau von Tatperson] gab
es allerdings auch bereits vor deren verhängnisvollen Bekanntschaft mit
[Name Vorname; männliches Opfer] zu verzeichnen. (*Bericht 41, Abs. 367*)]

A principal mechanism of the use of metaphors is to construct
homology—that is, to draw an analogy between the primary object,
the relationship, and the secondary object, the weather. The analogy in
this sense reveals how police writers see the relationship: If it is akin to
weather, it is like a natural force that cannot be influenced by humans.
Individuals have to face its inevitability and accept it as it is—be it sun-
shine or storm. Concerning the relationship, the reader is encouraged to
conclude that the partners cannot influence its development. The relationship acts on its own, and both partners are equally affected by its
deterioration.

An advantage of using metaphors consists in the catchy plausibility
the images supply. Without extensive reasoning readers appreciate—are
persuaded—that a fundamental change has taken place: "harmony" has
been replaced by "turbidity." The concept of relationship these contrasting
images reflect corresponds to a romantic and idealized notion of marital
relations. Sunny "blue marital skies" and "harmony" exclude active involvement, communication, friction, and debate as constitutive elements of a
relationship. Contrasting the case histories with a romantic idea of relationships allows police writers to depict the relationship between offender
and victim as in state of emergency—"weather vanes indicate storm." Considering the "fact" of such an emergency, it is less surprising, perhaps even
understandable, that the homicide took place.

Last but not least, the use of metaphors makes it possible to "say something without explicitly saying it"—without naming it. Metaphors allow

describing things that are conceived as negative or repulsive by using a different, harmless terminology instead. This euphemistic use of metaphors is applied in particular in regard to tabooed topics. Metaphoric phrasing enables police writers to describe "a bad relationship" without naming any of the facts that made the relationship bad—for instance, prior violence against the female partner. As we have demonstrated, reporting on violent behavior prior to the homicide rarely is part of the final investigation report. The favored use of metaphors instead points out the still present propensity—also among professionals—to keep one's distance from an uneasy, gendered problem; to ignore or normalize it; or even, to this day, to put violence against women by their partners under a taboo.

Conclusion

Analysis of language, text styles, and terminology used in police reports on domestic homicides proves a valuable and fruitful methodological approach to bring out institutional problem definition and prevalent interpretation patterns that direct investigation work and reporting of the police. Moreover, giving police reports as textual products a serious consideration by examining the chosen wording and the functioning of these texts is in our view an essential requirement, considering that further judicial institutions such as prosecution and courts strongly rely on these written police texts.

Language use present in the police reports on domestic homicides reveals specific—and far-reaching—characteristics and patterns:

- The more intimate a relationship is, the less the homicide is conceived as a crime. When reporting on homicides in intimate partnerships—mainly femicides—police avoid explicit terminology that points out the penal dimension. Instead, neutral wording, such as "the deed," predominates in these reports. In contrast, reporting about homicides between family members includes significantly more often terms that underline the seriousness of the incident ("crime," "murder").
- Prior violence against the female partner, the victim of the homicide, is not explicitly documented in intimate homicide reports. The choice of words in referring to prior incidents reflects an unawareness of violence against women and domestic violence as a background and significant interpretive ground for intimate homicides.

The concept of domestic violence is not present in the reports. Instead, vague descriptions and indeterminate hints summarize a "bad relationship." Remarkably enough, the perpetrator of prior violence most often is not designated at all. In contrast, grammatical phrasing of text sequences that—tacitly—deal with domestic violence feature depersonalizing passive forms and nominalizations. Wording transfers the active part not to the subjects involved but rather to "the relationship": it is the bad relationship that becomes an actor of its own. The preference for using metaphors to report on the relationship underlines the police writers' reluctance to be clear about antecedents, especially a history of domestic violence.

The language characteristics we have shown and the wording of police reports on domestic homicides constitute with regards to the criminal procedure an influencing factor not to underestimate. The fact, for instance, that terminology in the homicide reports does not reflect penal aspects of prior violence against the female partner contributes to a process of normalization and banalization—in other words, decriminalization—of domestic violence. The wording ignores the possibility of a connection between prior nonlethal domestic violence against the victim and the homicide under investigation, and thus keeps meaningful information from further judicial institutions. Moreover, actorless descriptions of a "bad relationship" construct a mutual situation for both perpetrator and victim. The phrasing ignores prior behavior or actions of the perpetrator and constructs the relationship as a factor of its own. Accordingly, language use in reporting downsizes the accountability of the perpetrator and establishes the "bad relationship" as a determining context of the homicide. Wording of the police presents the relationship as unfavorable circumstances for the perpetrator and consequently suggests the conditions of the relationship as an exculpatory factor. At the same time, reporting in no way frames prior domestic violence in words that document circumstances that may constitute an aggravating factor.

References

Block, Carolyn Rebecca, Judith M. McFarlane, Gail Rayford Walker, and Christine Ovcharchyn Devitt. (1999). "Beyond Public Records Databases: Field Strategies for Locating and Interviewing Proxi Respondents in Homicide Research." *Homicide Studies* 3 (4): 349–66.
Brookman, Fiona. (2005). *Understanding Homicide*. London: Sage.

Campbell, Jacquelyn C. (2001). "Risk Factors for Femicide in Abusive Relationships: Results from a Multi-Site Case Control Study." Abstract (unpublished).

Campbell, Jacquelyn C. et al. (2007). "Intimate Partner Homicide: Review and Implications of Research and Policy." *Trauma, Violence, and Abuse* 8 (3): 246–69.

Crocker, Diane. (2005). "Regulating Intimacy: Judicial Discourse in Cases of Wife Assault (1970 to 2000)." *Violence Against Women* 11 (197): 197–226.

Dawson, Myrna, and Rosemary Gartner. (1998). "Differences in the Characteristics of Intimate Femicides: The Role of Relationship State and Relationship Status." *Homicide Studies* 2 (4): 378–99.

Dobash, Rebecca Emerson et al. (2004). "Not an Ordinary Killer—Just an Ordinary Guy: When Men Murder an Intimate Woman Partner." *Violence Against Women* 10 (6): 577–605.

Dobash, Rebecca Emerson et al. (2007). "Lethal and Nonlethal Violence against an Intimate Female Partner: Comparing Male Murderers to Nonlethal Abusers." *Violence Against Women* 13 (4): 329–53.

Eisner, Manuel. (1997). *Das Ende der zivilisierten Stadt? Die Auswirkungen von Modernisierung und urbaner Krise auf Gewaltdelinquenz.* New York: Campus.

Gleixner, Ulrike. (1995). "Geschlechterdifferenzen und die Faktizität des Fiktionalen. Zur Dekonstruktion frühneuzeitlicher Verhörprotokolle." *WerkstattGeschichte* 11 (4): 65–70.

Gloor, Daniela, and Hanna Meier. (2009). *"Von der Harmonie zur Trübung"—Polizeiliche (Re-)Konstruktion von Tötungsdelikten im sozialen Nahraum: Eine qualitativ-soziologische Aktenuntersuchung.* Bern: Stämpli Verlag.

Gloor, Daniela, and Hanna Meier. (2011). "Culture and Ethnicity in (Re-)Constructing Domestic Homicides." In Monika Schröttle, Ravi K. Thiara, and Stéphanie A. Condon (eds.), *Violence against Women and Ethnicity: Commonalities and Differences across Europe*, 399–413. Opladen: Barbara Budrich Publishers.

Hoffmann, Ludger, ed. (1989). *Rechtsdiskurse: Untersuchungen zur Kommunikation in Gerichtsverfahren. Kommunikation und Institution 11.* Tübingen: Narr.

Hoffmann, Ludger. (1991). "Vom Ereignis zum Fall: Sprachliche Muster zur Darstellung und Überprüfung von Sachverhalten vor Gericht." In

Jörg Schönert (ed.), *Erzählte Kriminalität: Zur Typologie und Funktion von narrativen Darstellungen in Strafrechtspflege, Publizistik und Literatur zwischen 1770 und 1920*, 87–113. Tübingen: Max Niemeyer Verlag.

Innes, Martin. (2002). "Organizational Communication and the Symbolic Construction of Police Murder Investigations." *British Journal of Sociology* 53 (1): 67–87.

Innes, Martin. (2003). *Investigating Murder: Detective Work and the Police Response to Criminal Homicide*. Oxford: Oxford University Press.

Koch, Manfred. (2009). "Habe ich Genie, so werde ich Poete werden." Eine neue kritische Edition erschliesst und kommentiert Goethes Briefwerk. *Neue Zürcher Zeitung*, February 14–15, B3.

Löschper, Gabriele. (1999). *Bausteine für eine psychologische Theorie richterlichen Urteilens*. Baden-Baden: Nomos.

McFarlane, Judith M., Jacquelyn C. Campbell, Susan Wilt, Carolyn J. Sachs, Yvonne Ulrich, and Xiao Xu. (1999). "Stalking and Intimate Partner Femicide." *Homicide Studies* 3 (4): 300–316.

Meuser, Michael, and Reinhold Sackmann, eds. (1992). *Analyse sozialer Deutungsmuster: Beiträge zur empirischen Wissenssoziologie*. Pfaffenweiler: Centaurus.

Naucke, Wolfgang. (1991). "Die Stilisierung von Sachverhaltsschilderungen durch materielles Strafrecht und Strafprozessrecht." In Jörg Schönert (ed.), *Erzählte Kriminalität: Zur Typologie und Funktion von narrativen Darstellungen in Strafrechtspflege, Publizistik und Literatur zwischen 1770 und 1920*, 59–72. Tübingen: Max Niemeyer Verlag.

Nünning, Ansgar, ed. (2001). *Metzler Lexikon Literatur- und Kulturtheorie: Ansätze, Personen, Grundbegriffe*. Stuttgart: J. B. Metzler.

Polk, Kenneth. (1994). *When Men Kill: Scenarios of Masculine Violence*. Cambridge: Cambridge University Press.

Sauer, Christoph. (1989). "Der wiedergefundene Sohn: Diskursanalyse eines Strafverfahrens vor dem niederländischen 'Politierechter.'" In Hoffmann (ed.), *Rechtsdiskurse:Untersuchungen zur Kommunikation in Gerichtsverfahren. Kommunikation und Institution 11*, 63–128. Tübingen: Narr.

Schönert, Jörg, ed. (1991a). *Erzählte Kriminalität: Zur Typologie und Funktion von narrativen Darstellungen in Strafrechtspflege, Publizistik und Literatur zwischen 1770 und 1920*. Tübingen: Max Niemeyer Verlag.

Schönert, Jörg. (1991b). "Zur Einführung in den Gegenstandsbereich und zum interdisziplinären Vorgehen." InJörg Schönert (ed.), *Erzählte*

Kriminalität: Zur Typologie und Funktion von narrativen Darstellungen in Strafrechtspflege, Publizistik und Literatur zwischen 1770 und 1920, 11–55. Tübingen: Max Niemeyer Verlag.

Schwerhoff, Gerd. (1999). *Aktenkundig und gerichtsnotorisch: Einführung in die Historische Kriminalitätsforschung.* Tübingen: Edition Diskord.

Seibert, Thomas-Michael. (1981). *Aktenanalysen:Zur Schriftform juristischer Deutungen. Kommunikation und Institution 3.* Tübingen: Narr.

Silverman, David. (2006). *Interpreting Qualitative Data. Methods for Analyzing Talk, Text and Interaction,* Third Edition. London: Sage.

Smith, Dorothy E. (1983). "No One Commits Suicide: Textual Analysis of Ideological Practices." *Human Studies* 6 (1): 309–59.

Smith, Dwayne M., and Margret A. Zahn, eds. (1999). *Homicide: A Sourcebook of Social Research.* Thousand Oaks: Sage.

Smith, Paige Hall, Kathryne E. Moracco, and John D. Butts. (1998). "Partner Homicide in Context: A Population-Based Perspective." *Homicide Studies* 2 (4): 400–421.

Soeffner, Hans-Georg. (1989a). "Anmerkungen zu gemeinsamen Standards standardisierter und nicht-standardisierter Verfahren in der Sozialforschung." In Soeffner, *Auslegung des Alltags—der Alltag der Auslegung: zur wissenssoziologischen Konzeption einer sozialwissenschaftlichen Hermeneutik,* 51–65. Frankfurt a. M.: Suhrkamp.

Soeffner, Hans-Georg. (1989b). "Strukturanalytische Feldstudien: Ein Anwendungsbeispiel." In Soeffner, *Auslegung des Alltags—der Alltag der Auslegung: zur wissenssoziologischen Konzeption einer sozialwissenschaftlichen Hermeneutik,* 211–24. Frankfurt a. M.: Suhrkamp.

Starr, Kelly. (2008). *Covering Domestic Violence:A Guide for Journalist and Other Media Professionals.* Seattle: Washington State Coalition Against Domestic Violence.

Töngi, Claudia. (2004). *Um Leib und Leben:Gewalt, Konflikt, Geschlecht im Uri des 19. Jahrhunderts.* Zürich: Chronos.

Topalović, Elvira. (2003). *Sprachwahl—Textsorte—Dialogstruktur. Zu Verhörprotokollen aus Hexenprozessen des 17. Jahrhunderts.* Trier: Wissenschaftlicher Verlag Trier.

Wolff, Stephan. (2000). "Dokumenten- und Aktenanalyse." In Uwe Flick, Ernst von Kardorff, and Ines Steinke (eds.), *Qualitative Forschung, ein Handbuch,* 502–13. Reinbek bei Hamburg: Rowohlt.

Notes

1. The original study was conducted at the University of Basle, Switzerland, at the Center of Gender Studies, supported by the Swiss National Science Foundation (January 1, 2005–April 30, 2008). A comprehensive description of the research and its results is published in Gloor and Meier (2009).
2. Code of Criminal Procedure, Canton of Aargau, Switzerland (StPO, § 26, Abs. 1).
3. For an overview, see Smith and Zahn (1999); Brookman (2005). An exception is the work of Innes (2003), who examined homicide investigations from a symbolic interactionism viewpoint.
4. This matter primarily concerns the situation in the Swiss Canton Aargau, where this research was conducted, but it also is an issue in other Swiss places and other countries—for instance, Germany (Naucke 1991: 69). The common report guidelines of the Canton Aargau simply say," All police findings are to be recorded truthfully, precisely, objectively and clearly. Minor matters are to be excluded. Others' and own perceptions are to be distinguished" (Police of Canton Aargau, Report Doctrine, Order 048; translated by the authors). No further instructions are given.
5. The police report guidelines state that reports are "factual reports" and pass for "official statements" in the sense of "official documents" (*öffentliche Urkunde*): "According to the Civil Code art. 9 official documents enjoy the privilege of enhanced strength of evidence, which means it is assumed that the content of an official document conforms to facts and need not be given further proof" (Police of Canton Aargau, Report Guidelines: 2; translated by the authors). With this reference, the guidelines emphasize the central purpose of the documents—to function as "texts of truth." In this context Seibert mentions "two different language functions" that characterize institutional executions of records: "To inform members, and to convince non-members of its representation" (Seibert 1981: 32; translated by the authors).
6. See for instance the anthology "Erzählte Kriminalität" ("Narrated Criminality") that investigates rules and narrative forms of criminal justice texts (Schönert 1991a); as well Hoffmann (1989) and Löschper (1999). The development of such a perspective and its

significance for science of history is reflected in Schwerhoff (1999: 40ff.). For a discussion of the text type "court files" and records of other authorities, see also Topalović (2003: 97ff.).

7. See Naucke (1991: 65ff.).

8. Wolff conceives this challenge of so-called factual reports as a main focus for text and document analysis: those texts "have to evoke on the reader's side the impression of an objective and stable reality, yet simultaneously they have to hide the fact and mechanisms of their textual production and mediation"—that is, their being constructed (Wolff 2000: 508; translated by the authors).

9. "One of the most interesting and notable aspects of the police case files was how detectives tended to make use of the narrative form to organize their account of the crime. [. . .] The arrangement of the case material into a narrative form by the police needs to be under-stood as an artful construction, which purposively orders the incident in anticipation of the judicial stage of the criminal justice process. [. . .] As such, the narrative of the crime is not a "natural" feature of the event or police activity, but a social construction. Narratives are a device for configuring and representing reality in a particular way, they enable the author to present an account in a manner that provides sense-making connections between the people, places, objects and actions that contributed to the particular incident. [. . .] As 'knowledgeable' actors within the criminal justice system, the police are cognisant of the fact that the narrative is a persuasive form that meets juries' and other legal actors' 'common-sense' expectations of what they require to be able to understand a case" (Innes 2002: 78).

10. Using the example of Canadian courts, Crocker (2005) for instance demonstrates that judges' discourses often take up every-day stereotypes and strongly refer to traditional notions and gen-der models when discussing and assessing cases of wife assault (Crocker 2005).

11. Concerning the presence and validity of collective interpretation patterns in professional and everyday activities, see also Meuser and Sackmann (1992).

12. Sauer's discourse analysis of court proceedings demonstrates that "superordinate schemata" quite often take up "mystic, biblical and fairytale images" since "these models are well known and the most broadly accepted figures of description" and thus promote the

persuasive power of the account (Sauer 1989: 103; translated by the authors).

13. We may distinguish, for example, explicit and implicit elements or layers of texts. Text interpretation discusses and explores these also as "text—subtext" or as "latent" and "manifest" layers of texts (Nünning 2001).

14. From the institution's perspective, not only information concerning the incident (offense) is of interest to go on the record but also "institutional actions and writs [...] in order that third parties may extract from the document the formal course of proceedings" (Seibert 1981: 33; translated by the authors). Accounts of police actions are to be understood as confidence-building framework for the plot that ensures quality and reliability of the reconstructed happenings. The passages also serve as preventive action against possible (future) criticism of police investigation work. They also involve image management: police show off how their elaborate and circumspect work suited the case.

15. Final police reports on completed homicides cover an average of 42 pages, whereas those concerning attempted homicides comprise an average of 14 pages.

16. Investigations of completed homicides usually take more than seven months and up to a year as compared to half a month to three months for attempted cases. Investigations for three of the attempted homicides took only two weeks.

17. The Swiss criminal code distinguishes "murder" from "homicide": murder is specified by the fact that a perpetrator acts especially ruthlessly. That means notably the motive, the aim of the deed, or the style of performing are to be considered especially damnable (Art. 112 StGB). Therefore if the police writers, whose assignment does not comprise the legal definition and interpretation of the specific action under investigation but its description, make use of the term *murder* in reporting they imply a moral statement.

18. See for instance, Smith, Moracco, and Butts (1998); Dawson and Gartner (1998); McFarlane et al. (1999); Campbell (2001); Campbell (2007); Dobash et al. (2004); Dobash et al. (2007); Polk (1994); Block et al. (1999).

19. In her article "No One Commits Suicide: Textual Analysis of Ideological Practices," Dorothy Smith (1983) points out those processes

of active textual interaction and their persuasive effects on the reader's side.

20. Apart from "a bad relation" that constitutes the main concept in cases of intimate partner homicides, we also can distinguish the interpretation patterns of "personality" and the one of "alien cultural background" (see Gloor, Meier 2009: 223ff.). For the discussion of "alien cultural background" as a meaningful interpretation pattern in investigating intimate homicides, see Gloor and Meier (2011).

21. Latin roots of the term *conglomerate* (*conglomerare*) have the meaning of "massing together." In common parlance the term is used for the massing together of different materials into a new, distinct kind of substance.

22. The original report uses the term "Blessuren"—a rather old-fashioned general term for light wounds and scratches.

23. The use of weather metaphors by the police can be found also in other countries, as the following example shows: "He [the police chief] said the couple's tempestuous relationship could be to blame for the slaying" (*Seattle Times*, March 2, 2007; quoted in Starr 2008).

24. With the use of weather metaphors, police draw on a tradition that is well known to readers. The images promote, as "superordinate schemata" (Sauer 1989, see chapter 2.1), the persuasive power of the account. In regard to relationships, weather metaphors in particular have a strong literary tradition. Analysis of the extensive correspondence by Goethe for instance demonstrates his preference for weather metaphors: "A constant to be found throughout all the love affairs is the weather vanes–imagery for the heart" (Koch 2009; translated by the authors).

5

Talking about Violence

How People Convey Stereotypical Messages about Perpetrator and Victim through the Use of Biased Language

Anna Kwiatkowska, Poland

Introduction

This chapter examines how the use of abstract language can reinforce sexist stereotypes about gender and domestic violence against
women. The chapter first shows how gendered stereotypes operate in
Polish society, using indicative examples from the coverage of domestic
violence cases in the print media. These examples are analyzed in relation to Polish research on gender stereotypes including a discussion of
the scope (and limits) of the influence stereotypes can exert on assess-
ments of gender and domestic violence. This discussion then takes
into consideration social psychological research concerned with the
relationship between stereotyping and the level of abstractness of the
words used to characterize persons and events. This research suggests
that the kind of generalizations made in stereotypical statements—and
the falsehoods and biases these often imply—can be conveyed in subtle
ways without using blatantly obvious stereotypical remarks. However,
these issues have not yet been studied with regard to abstract language
use and domestic violence. Finally, new Polish research on the complex
interactions between gender, sexist stereotyping, and language use is
presented.

Beliefs about Violence and Gender Stereotypes

Popular opinion about violence against women, violence in close relationships, or domestic violence often has little to do with the reality of these relationships. People tend to underestimate the prevalence of abuse, do not always understand the dynamics of abusive relationships, tend to entertain false representations of perpetrators and their motives, and rarely understand the psyche of the victim. For example, in Poland it is widely believed that there is a direct causal link between alcohol consumption and violent behavior, which is expressed in a common saying about "a good husband" who "beats only when he drinks" (see Roszak 2008). Similarly, jealousy is often equated with love (and so is the controlling behavior often associated with possessive jealousy), and corporal punishment is widely accepted as a means of raising children.

Liz Kelly (1988) lists some of the most popular myths about sexual violence: "They enjoy/want it," "They ask for/deserve it," "It only happens to a certain type of women / in certain kinds of families," "They tell lies / exaggerate," "If they had resisted, they could have prevented it," "The men who do it are sick, ill, under stress, out of control." Adherence to such beliefs makes it difficult to recognize violence against women—the scale of the phenomenon and its prevalence, causes, dynamics, and consequences. Belief in such myths perpetuates a false image of women as objects of violence: passive, unable to defend themselves, hysteric, instigating violence, and lying. Such beliefs also divide women into those who presumably are never the object of violence and those who are thought to have some disposition to provoke violence. The myths described by Kelly also apply to men as perpetrators of violence, such as the belief that men can be easily provoked because of their assumed biological constitution (greater innate aggressiveness, greater demand for sex). It is also a myth that violence is only perpetrated by people with specific pathological characteristics—for example, sexual deviants and psychopaths.

Anna Kwiatkowska (1998) analyzed the relationship between gender stereotypes and beliefs about domestic violence. The sample in this study consisted of 198 women and 94 men aged 19–50. Based on factor analyses of quantitative questionnaire data, Kwiatkowska identified nine types of belief: (1) opinions legitimizing domestic violence, (2) beliefs in the existence of violence only in certain environments, (3) beliefs about the prevalence of domestic violence, (4) beliefs about emotional or personality disorders in the perpetrator, (5) beliefs about the disciplining function of violent actions, (6) beliefs about the role of the environment in incidents of violence, (7) beliefs in the lack of religiosity as a source of violence, (8) beliefs that women like it, and (9) beliefs that violence is not the only means of resolving conflicts.

In addition, the study found that gender stereotypes are good predictors of some of these beliefs but not of other beliefs. More specifically, beliefs that legitimize domestic violence reflect a particular notion of gendered intrafamily relations, and of relations between women and men, in which the woman and other family members depend on the man and accept what he does (for a detailed description of the findings, see Kwiatkowska, 1998, s. 138–42). These convictions can be expected in people who are attached to the image of man as the father of the family. Women, even more so than men, who subscribe to this notion, tend to justify a man's actions in the family and grant him the right to enforce obedience from the family members, including the use of violence. This type of dependence on a male head of family is consistent with patriarchal values that are still held in much of Polish society.

In a similar vein, the belief that domestic violence occurs only in certain social environments can be predicted from the acceptance of culturally specific stereotypical images of men and women such as "Father of the Family," "Gentleman," "Polish Mother," and "Lady." The idealized image (mostly held by women) of men as respectable family fathers and gentlemen, and the equally idealized image (mostly held by men) of women as caring mothers and elegant ladies, is the reason domestic violence is seen only in circumstances where these ideals are not met—namely, in marginalized environments and among people who are less educated and relatively poor. The question then arises of how women and men in these environments are perceived. The answer lies in a well-known cultural dichotomy of gender stereotypes: If women are not ladies, then they must be sluts. If men are not gentlemen, then they must be brutes.

Furthermore, in this study the belief that violence results from specific (mostly pathological) characteristics of the perpetrator was associated, perhaps surprisingly, with the stereotype of the devoted and caring "Polish Mother" who dedicates herself to her family. Perhaps those who hold this image associate domestic violence with some kind of weakness in the offender, which can be justified and forgiven by the good and caring Polish Mother. The image of the Polish Mother has particular connotations within Polish society. It is associated with the repeated historical experience of Polish uprisings against foreign occupations, during which women, in addition to being mothers, were often the sole providers for their families. These historical experiences are sometimes expressed in heroic narratives of the (distant and recent) past through which images of the Polish Mother are imbued with heightened significance for Polish history and identity.

However, Kwiatkowska (1998) also found that some beliefs about domestic violence were not related to gender stereotypes. The conviction that violence can occur anywhere, not just at the so-called margins of society, along with the belief that domestic violence persists in environments that are unresponsive and permissive, had no relation to what respondents thought about women and men in general. Instead, other factors seemed more important in predicting acceptance of such beliefs, including general knowledge about society and more specific knowledge about the origins and dynamics of domestic violence.

How important is holding certain stereotypes and beliefs about violence for the functioning of individuals, groups, and social systems? Is it worth analyzing the symbolic behavior in this area when people involved in violence expect actual help and real, not symbolic actions?In other words, what are the practical consequences of the persistence of such beliefs in society?

When defining a stereotype, Walter Lippman's remark about a "picture in the head" (Stangor and Schaller 1996) is often cited. Cognitive social psychologists have adopted a similar perspective. In this view stereotypes are seen as part of the information processing that happens in the head of an individual. Stereotypes are considered cognitive representations of a group such as women, men, perpetrators, or victims. In a different perspective influenced by Edwin Hutchins (1996, quoted in Semin 2008), Gün Semin argued that stereotypes ought to be seen in the context of communication and social interaction, and moved from the private sphere into the public sphere. When stereotypes are studied only as cognitive phenomena, and analyzed only in terms of cognitive processes, it is difficult to see their social functions and the relationship between cognition and action. Thus an exclusive focus on cognition would make it harder to notice the relationship between, for instance, the stereotype of father as family patriarch (cognitive element) and the failure to intervene in domestic violence (action element). Therefore, in order to move from passive witnessing of domestic violence to active intervention, representations of violence, perpetrators, and victims need to change. The relationship between cognition and representation can be demonstrated in media reporting about domestic violence.

Representation of Domestic Violence in Polish Media

The power of the media stems from at least two facts: they provide and disseminate information and they select and evaluate this information and thereby convey a specific view of the world. Given the number of events that could be presented in the media, selection among them is inevitable. As events are represented they also are evaluated. The mere fact of being selected for reporting makes an event appear important—it has become "newsworthy." In addition, evaluation is included in the way the event is presented.

In January 2006, the weekly magazine *Przekrój* published an article discussing the problem of violence in the families of police officers. Police officers who are violent toward members of their own families often go unpunished. The victims do not call the police because they assume that the police are the perpetrator's colleagues and will side with him. Even when abused families seek help, they are unlikely to receive it. In the following example, the wife of a police officer reported to the police that her husband beat his daughter. "When the father had beaten his pregnant daughter the mother went to complain to the supervisor of her husband. The response: 'Mrs. Krysia, your daughter had a one-night stand and her father can't even give her a slap?'" (*Przekrój*, January 5, 2006).

The response of the supervisor reframes the entire incident. First, the daughter is turned from victim into perpetrator (having had reprehensible, casual sex, she ought to be punished). In addition, the father is no longer a perpetrator of violence but—within the patriarchal moral order—he is called on to execute justice. He almost appears to be a victim of circumstance, as he is forced to use corporal punishment against his daughter. Finally, the beating is reduced to "giving a slap," with slapping being one of the commonly used and widely accepted means of disciplining children.

With this reframing the supervisor accomplished several things at once. He downplayed the event by minimizing the physical aspect of it and reducing it to an insignificant slap. He changed the nature of the relationship between perpetrator and victim from one between two adults to one between father and child. Finally, the supervisor reversed the moral judgment of the incident by blaming the daughter rather than the father. Thus the act of physical violence—as interpreted by the supervisor—ceases to be reprehensible conduct (hitting a pregnant woman) and becomes a meritorious deed that restores the moral order (father chastising his wayward daughter). It is in vain to expect intervention on behalf of the daughter from a person who sees the world in these categories.

Another widespread belief about domestic violence is related to the contexts in which violence presumably occurs, such as particular social groups, environments, or places. Opinions about the occurrence of violence are shaped by media messages that stress specific characteristics of the environment in which the reported event occurred or to which the participants in the incident belong. For example, the tabloid *Fakt* reported on September 11, 2008, "We heard a story of a monster from the Podlasie region who for 6 years raped his daughter and abused his family. As we found out, he himself comes from a family in which violence was a part of everyday life and the evil has accompanied him since childhood. He stole, skipped school and hurt people" (*Fakt*, September 11, 2008).

For those who believe that violence occurs only in "other" marginalized or crime-ridden contexts, it is easier to believe that there will be no violence in their own contexts and that the problem is of no further concern. Dividing the world into "we, the good ones" and "they, the bad ones" helps keep "them" at a distance. By adopting such a stance, violence in one's own environment is more easily overlooked, and signals, which in a different context might be considered alarming, are interpreted differently. This conviction about the "integrity" of one's own environment is sustained by the myths and stereotypes of the Polish gentleman and protective father, the caring mother, and the "holy" family. Hence the shock and outrage evident in the news reports when disgusting practices of fathers, mothers, sons, and daughters come to light: "they were maltreated by *their own* mother" (*Fakt*, April 6, 2009); "he raped *his own* daughter and maltreated *his own* family" (*Fakt*, September 11, 2008); "for years she tormented *her own* mother" (*Przekrój*, January 5, 2006; my emphasis).

Maintaining the intellectual and emotional distance from the phenomenon of domestic violence is also facilitated by the belief that perpetrators are often people with pathological personality or other psychological defects. The media sustain such opinions by using terms such as *Polish Fritzl, madman, Iranian pervert, tyrant, monster, psychopath, sadist.*

However, there is another side to the coin. If the source of the violence is seen in some deficiency attributed to the offender that is considered fixed and not caused by him, then his ability to control his behavior is considered compromised. He then is credited with less culpability or even absolved. For instance, in Polish society when a crime is committed by a drunken person, it is treated with greater indulgence, as if the alcohol and not the man was the culprit. It must be noted that the alcohol excuse is only granted to men, not to women.

In the preceding press quotations, beliefs about violence and opinions about perpetrators and victims are expressed in a blatant way. Readers are likely to have few doubts about the intentions of news reporters who invoke "hell" or "degenerate mothers"; the stereotyping seems obvious and the goal appears to be to stoke up strong emotions in the readers. Readers have the option, at least in principle, to deliberately accept or reject this view of the world.

However, when subtle language is used, it may be difficult to recognize the impact of a message, and the audience may assimilate the authors' point of view, stereotypes, and emotional response without being fully aware that they are doing so. This can happen when words with specific formal features are chosen. One of these features, which will be discussed in the remainder of this chapter, is abstractness. In particular, when the goal is to share controversial information or express controversial beliefs, it is easier to use abstract language than to give concrete facts (Anolli, Zurloni, and Riva 2006). The impact of abstract language is also considerable when another person is described with whom the listener has no direct acquaintance. Abstract language conveys the speaker's assessment of the person without supplying concrete detail from which the listener could form an opinion. In this way, the listener may form a mental image of a person whom she has never met merely based on suggestions implied by abstract language. Thus abstract language can be an indicator of hidden meanings that are not explicitly stated.

Abstract Language and the Maintenance of Stereotypes

Given current political correctness in Poland, it is rare to hear politicians express blatant prejudice in public without suffering public reprimand and suspicions that they are a racist, sexist, or religious fundamentalist (politically incorrect speech may be more common in the tabloid press and on

Internet forums). When politicians voice opinions such as "a wife should obey her husband," "it's impossible to raise kids without a sound spanking from time to time," "don't wash your dirty laundry in public," or "a woman's place is in the kitchen," they encounter an indignant reaction from progressive circles. It was therefore highly unusual to hear a statement like "At least we know that our husbands are real men," which was delivered by the wife of a politician who was accused of sexually harassing and raping women who were employees and subordinates in his businesses.

However, there are ways to express controversial opinions without risking one's reputation. The preceding statement by the politician's wife framed sexual promiscuity (and sexual harassment and rape) as accepted behavior of a real man, which is consistent with the stereotype of a macho male. The same sentiment can be expressed differently, using structural properties of language. For example, having sexual intercourse with many women can be framed in different ways, as the following two sets of statements show:

(a) He slept with a woman.   (a') He slept with a woman.

(b) He teased a woman.   (b') He abused a woman.

(c) He likes women.   (c') He hates women.

(d) He is seductive.   (d') He is uncontrollable.

(e) He is a real man.   (e') He is a rapist.

Statements in the first group carry relatively positive connotations, whereas statements in the second group are increasingly negative. More important, in each set the statements vary from concrete to abstract, and from being relatively descriptive to implying, invoking, or alluding. Although all the expressions relate to having sex with a woman, some expressions refer to sex directly, whereas others may have quite distant connections with sex or none at all. What are the reasons for choosing one of these statements and refusing another?

According to Semin (2012) the main function of language is to focus attention, and this focusing of attention is used for specific purposes. If the aim of a communicator is to focus the listener or reader's attention on a person, expressions like those in (d), (d'), (e), and (e') are likely to be chosen. In contrast, if the aim is to focus attention on the situational context, expressions like those in (a) and (a') are likely to be chosen. Finally, when a speaker or writer wants to focus attention on the object of a behavior, in this case a woman, he or she is more likely to choose an expression like those in (c) and (c'). Thus the selection of words or expressions reflects interpersonal goals that are accomplished by strategically (although not necessarily consciously) using words or expressions at different levels of abstractness, with expressions in (a) and (a') the most concrete and those in (e) and (e') the most abstract.

Episodes described in concrete language are, at least in principle, easier to verify than episodes described in abstract language (for instance, verifying the occurrence of sexual intercourse versus verifying whether somebody is a real man). This matters for causal explanations of behavior. Whether causes of a given behavior are attributed to situational factors or to inner dispositions has important consequences for how an actor and his or her responsibility for the behavior are perceived. Furthermore, people who talk about positive behavior performed by somebody close to them such as a friend, partner, or member of their in-group tend to choose abstract terms, which has the effect of emphasizing that the behavior is typical of the friend's positive character. In contrast, if the friend did something wrong, people are more likely to use concrete terms, which has the effect of emphasizing that the wrongdoing was out of character.

Thus, when the wife of the politician who sexually harassed his female subordinates uses a positive, abstract term such as "real man," she attempts to reframe his acts as evidence of "great" personality. Had she been ashamed of his behavior, she might have chosen a concrete term (*"He slept with a woman, so what?"*) to emphasize that the behavior was an uncharacteristic faux pas. Yet, had she wanted to malign a rival politician accused of the same behavior, she might have chosen a negative, abstract term to emphasize that the act was evidence of despicable personality.

This reasoning about the role of abstract language in interpersonal communication is developed more formally in the Linguistic Category Model (LCM) by Gün Semin and Klaus Fiedler (1991). This model has gained strong empirical support in social psychology. Its basic principles are explained here briefly (for a full account see Semin and Fiedler 1988;1989).

LCM is a model of language use in interpersonal communication that explains when specific words and expressions are used to make assertions about social events and people. According to Semin (2000; Semin and Fiedler 1991) different linguistic forms can activate specific cognitive patterns concerning the perception and evaluation of actions, including perceived causality, responsibility, and ability to be in control. In addition, such linguistic forms may induce specific emotions regardless of the mean-ing of the words used. The main idea is that the same behavioral episode can be encoded at four different levels of abstraction (Semin and Fiedler 1988; Brown and Fish 1983).

At the most concrete level are so-called descriptive action verbs ("A is talking to B"; "A slept with a woman"). They assert concrete, observable behaviors with a beginning and an end. Without further contextual infor-mation, descriptive action verbs are relatively unambiguous, neutral in value, and leave little room for interpretation.

At the next level are interpretive action verbs ("A is helping B"; "A teased a woman"; "B abused a woman"). They are less concrete and more open to interpretation. In contrast to descriptive action verbs, interpreta-tive verbs assert meaning attributed to behavior. According to Semin and Fiedler (1988), "There exists an abundance of verbs that fulfill not only a function of behavior classification and discrimination (from other behav-iors) but also interpretation, eg. encourage, mislead, cheat, flatter, threaten etc." (559). The interpretation of both descriptive and interpretive verbs depends on context.

More abstract are verbs referring to states ("A likes B"; "A likes women"; "B hates women"). State verbs assert a psychological state of person A in relation to person B. They no longer reference behavior (in the sense of what A is doing to B). Assertions made by state verbs may be difficult or impossible to verify. State verbs assert relatively enduring subjective emo-tional, motivational, or cognitive states that may be expressed in any num-ber of concrete actions.

At the most abstract level are adjectives ("A is an extroverted person"; "A is seductive"; "B is uncontrollable."). Adjectives make assertions without reference to specific behaviors and contexts, and without reference to the person at whom behavior might be directed. In the example, the adjective is used to distinguish person A from other persons who are not extroverted, and thus classify person A in relation to others in terms of extroversion. Adjectives such as honest, impulsive, reliable, helpful, and creative describe highly abstract characteristics that provide generalizations across specific behavioral events, situations, and interaction partners.

Other scholars have expanded this model by including nouns at a fifth level of abstraction. For example, in research on political discourse, Anolli, Zurloni, and Riva (2006) argued for nouns as most abstract forms to make assertions about persons because nouns are used mainly to include a person in a social category. An abstract noun could comprise a wide range of concrete behaviors without explicitly mentioning them. This opens a linguistic passage, so to speak, through which stereotypical notions may slip into the reader's or listener's processing of the information ("A is a real man"; "B is a rapist"). In short, according to the Linguistic Category Model, verbs, adjectives, and nouns can be thought of along a continuum of abstractness with descriptive action verbs at the concrete end and nouns at the abstract end.

The degree of abstractness of the words used in a message has significant implications for interpersonal communication. First, abstract expressions make the relationship between an action and the situation in which it occurred more ambiguous while also implying relatively stable behavioral tendencies over time. Second, abstract words are more relevant to the personality of a person and imply that he or she has relatively less deliberate control over their behavior. Thus using abstract expressions implies and invites causal attributions for behaviors that are relatively stable over time and global across situations. The cause of a behavioral episode can thus be situated within factors over which the actor is thought to have little control, such as by explaining violent actions with the perpetrator's bad temper or aggressiveness, or in relation to the characteristics of the victim (e.g., the child is unbearable; the child provoked him). In other words, the use of action verbs draws attention to the specific details of an event, whereas the use of state verbs, adjectives, and nouns draws attention to general characteristics of the actor.

The Linguistic Category Model was developed mainly to illuminate processes that operate unconsciously in person perception and the attribution of causality for behaviors or events. In addition, the concrete-abstract dimension has been employed in the analysis of intergroup relations and descriptions of the behavior of in-group and out-group members. In particular, antagonism toward the out-group and favoritism toward the in-group tends to be expressed at different levels of abstraction in conjunction with positive or negative valence (Schmid 1999). This phenomenon is known as linguistic intergroup bias (LIB; Maass 1999; Wigboldus and Douglas 2007).

Linguistic intergroup bias refers to the tendency to use higher levels of abstraction (i.e., generalization) when encoding and communicating desirable (positive) behavior of the in-group and undesirable (negative) behavior of the out-group. For example, behaviors in which help is offered to members of an in-group might be described as expressions of altruism—a stable personality trait characteristic of a person, whereas the same behaviors by an out-group member might be described in more concrete terms without generalizing beyond a given situation and without implying that the out-group member is a helpful person.

Similarly, negative behaviors are encoded at a higher level of abstraction when the person belongs to an out-group and not to the in-group. For example, aggressive behaviors are more often attributed to stable characteristics of a member of an out-group (thus branding the person as an aggressive individual), whereas when the member of an in-group is aggressive the event is described in more concrete terms that make the behavior appear situation-specific and atypical (Maass, Salvi, Arcuri, and Semin 1989; Maass and Arcuri 1996).

Two different psychological mechanisms have been hypothesized that may underlie this differential use of abstract language. One mechanism assumes in-group identity protective motives based on the Social Identity Theory. Daniël Wigboldus, Gün Semin, and Russell Spears (2006) showed that speakers construct messages at more abstract levels when they transmit information that is consistent with a stereotype. Furthermore, stereotype-consistent messages make the recipient draw conclusions about dispositions more often than messages that are stereotype inconsistent. The second mechanism may be related to expectations rather than identity protection. Expected behaviors (that are consistent with a stereotype) are described with abstract language, and unexpected behaviors with concrete terms (Semin 2012).

The research discussed so far suggests that interpersonal relations are influenced, to some extent, by assertions of what a person has done to another person. Depending on the level of abstractness, such assertions appear to modify the amount of control actors are perceived to have over their behavior. Such assertions may appear accurate and unbiased, and not smack of stereotype and prejudice. And yet, they also convey implicit understandings of what happened and whether what happened was positive or negative. Such use of language means that the speaker (or writer) is able to convey important feelings and evaluations in an indirect way that removes evaluative components of a message, along with possible biases, from open discussion. As a result, we may not be able to indicate the source of feelings and evaluations generated by the assertion. What has been said is, at face level, politically correct, while still evoking implicit positive or negative stereotypes (Semin 2008).

Furthermore, people whose positive behavior is described with abstract terms and whose negative behavior is described with concrete terms tend to feel closer to the person who is depicting them, whereas people whose behavior is described in concrete terms when positive and in abstract terms when negative tend to feel more distant from the person who is describing them.

Structural properties of language, such as concreteness-abstractness, can be helpful for conveying indirectly a sense of social distance between the speaker and the actors in an event (Semin 2008). When stereotypes are imbedded in an assertion in this way, the recipient of the message may not be aware of the cause of feelings he or she is beginning to experience. Indeed, the sender may also be unaware that he or she uses stereotypes in communicating. Empirical data show that people do not necessarily have conscious access to biases that occur in the language they use and may not be aware of their biases in constructing their speech (Semin 2008; Douglas and Sutton 2006).

Endorsement of stereotypes tends to increase such unconscious use of abstract terms. Choice of abstract or concrete language is not controlled consciously but managed by processes to which the speaker usually has no conscious access. This also means that the accessibility of cultural stereotypes about the topic in question tends to increase the use of abstract language.

However, the tendency to use abstract language does not necessarily reflect a person's individual stereotypes. As previously mentioned, abstract language may be motivated by a desire to defend one's social identity when an out-group is perceived to threaten the in-group (Maass, Ceccarelli, and Rudin 1996). Anne Maass et al. showed that groups who feel their identity is threatened use language that favors their in-group. Specifically, these groups describe positive behaviors of in-group members more abstractly and their negative behaviors more concretely. Another motive for the use of abstract language concerns the need for cognitive closure or certainty— that is, a preference for assured and unequivocal statements or opinions. Those who have a high need for certainty show a general tendency for more abstract descriptions of people (Webster, Kruglanski, and Pattison 1997; Douglas, Sutton, and McGarty 2008). In an examination of this tendency in a legal context, Jeannette Schmid et al. (1996) showed that prosecutors typically use more abstract language to describe activities of the accused, which emphasizes the personal responsibility or criminal disposition of the accused.

Applications and Limitations of the Linguistic Category Model

The model has been used to examine how abstract language influences stereotyping (Maass 1999; Maass et al. 1992; 1995; 2006) and whether it introduces bias into responses to questions (Semin 1995). It has been used in studies on perceived social proximity (Reitsma-van Rooijen, Semin, and van Leeuwen 2007) and to explore differences between adjectives and nouns as sources of stereotyping (Maass, Corvino, and Arcuri 1994; Graf, Bilewicz, Finell, and Geschke 2013). Other research has focused on determinants of abstract language use such as need for cognitive closure (Rubini and Krug-lanski 1997). Determinants and consequences of language abstractness have been studied in a range of social contexts, including relationships between political parties, among interest groups, between the sexes, in competition among schools and sport teams, in courtrooms, and in the language of sports journalists (for a review, see Maass and Arcuri 1992).

Within the context of LCM research, structural properties of language have been investigated mainly for Standard English, but similar findings have been obtained in other languages as well, including German, Italian, and Dutch. A study by Sylvie Graf et al. (2013) was carried out with German, Polish, Finnish, and Czech samples. The levels of abstraction identified by the Linguistic Category Model have been documented in English, Italian, German, and Spanish (Semin 2008). However, Anne Maass, Minoru Karasawa, Federica Politi, and Sayaka Suga (2006) showed that Japanese preferred to use concrete language (i.e., verbs) over abstract language (i.e., adjectives). The model has also been used—albeit with varying degrees of success—in Polish.

However, to this author's knowledge, there is no research examining the usefulness of the model for researching interpersonal, gendered violence. The study by Agata Bruj (2010) presented next breaks new ground.

LCM as a Theoretical Framework for
Studies on Violence against Women

Bruj used the model to examine determinants of abstract language use in assertions about domestic violence against women. Although the model seems to have some cross-language validity, some cultural specificity was found as well.

Bruj (2010) used an experimental design to determine whether the level of abstraction preferred for assertions about domestic violence cases depends on the gender of the people who communicate the case and the level of sexist attitudes they hold. Three research questions were asked: What are the preferences regarding the choice of level of language abstractness in the description of violent acts toward women? Do men have different preferences compared to women? What is the role of hostile and benevolent sexism in the use of different levels of abstractness?

For the role of gender, it was predicted that the level of abstraction would depend on whether study participants perceived the perpetrator as a member of their in-group. As most cases of the kind of domestic violence portrayed in the study's case vignettes is perpetrated by men against women, it was expected that male participants would consider the perpetrator as one of their in-group, whereas female participants would consider him as a member of the out-group. According to the predictions of the Linguistic Expectation Bias (LEB; Maass, Milesi, Zabbini, Stahlberg 1995) abstract language is used to describe in-group members and people we like in positive terms, and to describe out-group members and people we dislike in negative terms. Thus it was predicted that male participants would use concrete language to describe violent behavior of another man, whereas female respondents would use abstract language.

Regarding the effects of sexism, a stereotypical image of women in terms of hostile sexism would be woman as temptress and provocateur, whereas a stereotypical image of women in terms of benevolent sexism would be virtuous and weak female (Glick and Fiske 1996). It was predicted that the tendency to use abstract terms will depend on the form of sexism. More specifically, it was assumed that participants with higher levels of hostile sexism would blame the female victim and excuse the male perpetrator and therefore prefer concrete language in assertions about male perpetrators. In contrast, participants with higher levels of benevolent sexism were expected to condemn the violent behavior of the man and use abstract terms. In this case, the line of reasoning by a benevolent sexist may be as follows: A man should not behave in such a way because a woman is a fragile and delicate creature, in need of protection by a strong and powerful man. If he is violent toward her, there is something wrong with the man, not the woman. Therefore a benevolent sexist would be expected to refer to inner dispositions of the perpetrator and prefer abstract language to describe the event.

A total of 248 individuals participated in the study: 135 women and 113 men. The age of participants ranged from 18 to 55, with an average age of 25. Of respondents, 48 percent had some higher education, and 42 percent had finished secondary school. The study was conducted via the Internet with an online questionnaire. The respondents read three vignettes each describing an incident of domestic violence against women.

As an example,

> As he does every day, Marek, 40, construction worker and resident of Praga [a neighborhood in Warsaw], came home from work Tuesday evening around 7 o'clock. Marta, his wife, was busy putting their son to bed. When Marek entered the house, Marta was reading a fairy tale to little Jas. Marek burst into the child's room, dragged Marta into the kitchen and showed her a stain on the floor made by spilled milk. He shouted he did not understand how it could be that a woman, sitting all day at home and doing nothing, did not care to keep the house clean and tidy. He requested she clean it immediately. When Marta said she would want to put little Jas to bed first, Marek punched her in her face, and said that it was her primary duty to obey her husband, and she would better do as she was told. Marta, tears running down her face, started to clean the floor.

The perceived severity of the abuse was similar for all three vignettes. As there were no significant differences between them, means were averaged across the three vignettes.

To measure the dependent variable "preference for abstractness," each vignette was followed by four statements about the vignette that reflected the four levels of abstraction: "A resident of Praga punched his wife" (most concrete; descriptive action verb), "A resident of Praga hurt his wife" (somewhat concrete; interpretive action verb), "A resident of Praga hates his wife" (somewhat abstract; state verb), "A resident of Praga is aggressive" (most abstract; adjective). The respondents were asked to indicate on a five-point scale the extent to which each of four sentences best describes the given event.

The independent variables were sex of participant and level of ambivalent sexism measured with the Polish adaptation of the Ambivalent Sexism Scale by Peter Glick and Susan Fiske (1996). Results revealed that, in general, interpretive verbs were preferred, followed by adjectives (Figure 5.1). The differences in preference for interpretive verbs over descriptive verbs and over state verbs were statistically significant, as were the differences between preference for adjectives over descriptive verbs and over state verbs. Preferences for descriptive verbs and state verbs were not statistically different (Friedman's $\chi2$ (3) = 166, 0; p=0.00).

As predicted, compared to men, women preferred abstract language in assertions about the perpetrator (adjectives; ADJ: F>M Test U: p<0.02; Figure 5.2).

Furthermore, women's sexist attitudes were not related to preference for abstract language, but for men, benevolent sexism was (Figure 5.3). Male participants who endorsed benevolent sexism preferred abstract assertions about the perpetrator (state verbs and adjectives; ADJ by Sexism: $\chi2$ (2) = 7, 85; p< 0.02; SV by Sexism: $\chi2$ (2) = 5, 70; p< 0.05).

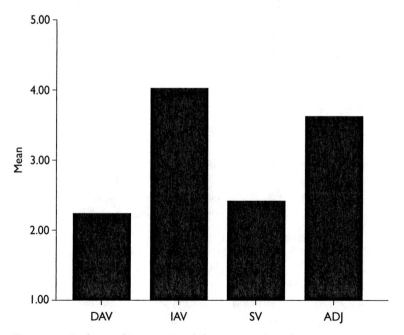

Figure 5.1   Preference for concrete and abstract assertions about perpetrator
Note: DAV=Descriptive action verbs; IAV=Interpretive action verbs; SV=State verbs; ADJ=Adjectives.

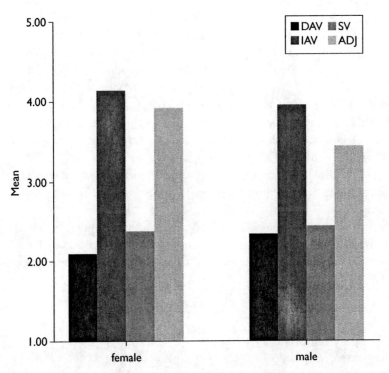

Figure 5.2   Women and men's preference for abstract assertions about perpetrator

The results of this study show that the Linguistic Category Model can provide a useful tool for studying language used in statements about domestic violence against women. In assertions about violent incidents, people may prefer abstract language because it allows them to interpret the incidents in terms of a broader class of behaviors and to locate causes of the behavior in stable characteristics of the perpetrator. At the same time, this preference may generate stereotypical framings of such incidents.

In the study by Bruj, women were more likely than men to prefer abstract language for characterizing incidents of domestic violence. According to the linguistic-intergroup-bias rationale, one reason for this preference might be that the perpetrator is seen as a member of an outgroup, displaying stereotypical out-group behavior. For men, benevolent sexism was associated with a preference for abstract language. A man who adopts attitudes of benevolent sexism believes in a special relationship between the sexes in which women are wonderful but vulnerable creatures

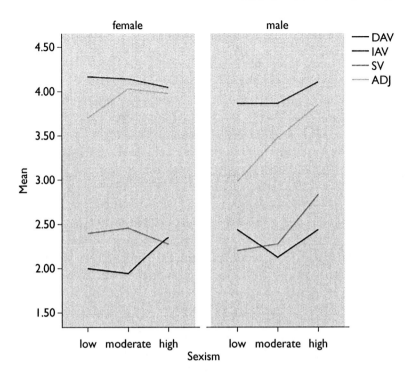

Figure 5.3   Men's benevolent sexism and preference for abstract assertions about perpetrator

who need men's protection. Thus harsh treatment of women is performed only by "lunatics" and "brutes"—not by "normal" men of the in-group. In this case, abstract language would serve as a tool for male participants to socially distance themselves from violent men and exclude them from the in-group. It is unclear why for women sexist attitudes were not associated with preference for abstract language. Perhaps women are more inclined to see domestic violence as an unambiguous event, irrespective of any subjective factors.

Concluding Remarks

The research discussed in this chapter may have practical uses for intervention in domestic violence against women. Two potential applications are suggested here: as a tool for women and their supporters that can help them to explore tendencies to blame the victim and excuse the perpetrator, and as a tool for teaching students about domestic violence and violence against women.

The research suggests that it would be helpful to explain the powerful influence of concrete and abstract language. In particular, it may help to deliberately avoid describing (and thus excusing) the perpetrator in concrete terms and instead to describe him in abstract terms to see the generalized patterns of his abuse. This recommendation could be built into advice literature or workshops for women, their supporters, and professionals such as nurses, doctors, teachers, and social workers who may encounter female victims of domestic violence.

Second, the research may inform techniques for teaching students about domestic violence and violence against women. It might be a good exercise for pupils and students to learn to pay attention to the level of abstractness of the language used in media reports and politicians' statements, and perhaps in students' own assertions about domestic violence when making statements about victims and perpetrators.

References

Anolli, L., V. Zurloni, and G. Riva. (2006). "Linguistic Intergroup Bias in Political Communication." *Journal of General Psychology* 1933: 237–55.

Brown, R., and D. Fish. (1983). "The Psychological Causality Implicit in Language." *Cognition* 14: 233–74.

Bruj, A. (2010). "Level of Language Abstractness in Talking about Domestic Violence." Unpublished MA Thesis, Warsaw School of Social Sciences and Humanities.

Douglas, K. M., and R. M. Sutton. (2006). "When What You Say about Others Says Something about You: Language Abstraction and Inferences about Describers' Attitudes and Goals." *Journal of Experimental Social Psychology* 42: 500–508.

Douglas, K. M., R. M. Sutton, and C. McGarty. (2008). "Strategic Language Use in Interpersonal and Intergroup Communication." In Y. Kashima, K. Fiedler, and P. Freytag (eds.), *Stereotype Dynamics: Language-Based Approaches to the Formation, Maintenance, and Transformation of Stereotypes*, 189–212. New York: Lawrence Erlbaum Associates.

Glick, P., and S. T. Fiske. (1996). "The Ambivalent Sexism Inventory: Differentiating Hostile and Benevolent Sexism." *Journal of Personality and Social Psychology* 3: 491–512.

Graf, S., M. Bilewicz, E. Finell, and D. Geschke. (2013). "Nouns Cut Slices: Effects of Linguistic Forms on Intergroup Bias." *Journal of Language and Social Psychology* 32: 62–83.

Kelly, L. (1988). *Surviving Sexual Violence.* Minneapolis: University of Minnesota Press.

Kwiatkowska, A. (1998). "Gender Stereotypes and Beliefs about Family Violence in Poland." In R. C. Klein (ed.), *Multidisciplinary Perspectives on Family Violence*, 129–52. London: Routledge.

Maass, A. (1999). "Linguistic Intergroup Bias: Stereotype Perpetuation through Language." In M. P. Zanna (ed.), *Advances in Experimental Social Psychology*, Vol. 31, 79–121. San Diego: Academic Press.

Maass, A., and L. Arcuri. (1992). "The Role of Language in the Persistence of Stereotypes." In G. Semin and K. Fiedler (eds.), *Language, Interaction, and Social Cognition*, 129–43. Newbury Park, CA: Sage.

Maass, A., and L. Arcuri. (1996). "Language and Stereotyping." In C. N. Macrae, C. Stangor, and M. Hewstone (eds.), *Stereotypes and Stereotyping*, 193–226. New York: Guilford Press.

Maass, A. S., L. Arcuri, and G. Semin. (1989). "Language Use in Intergroup Contexts: The Linguistic Intergroup Bias." *Journal of Personality and Social Psychology* 57: 981–93.

Maass, A., R. Ceccarelli, and S. Rudin. (1996). "Linguistic Intergroup Bias: Evidence for an In-Group Protective Motivation." *Journal of Personality and Social Psychology* 71: 116–26.

Maass, A., P. Corvino, and L. Arcuri. (1994). "Linguistic Intergroup Bias and the Mass Media." *Revue Internationale de Psychologie Sociale* 1: 31–43.

Maass, A., M. Karasawa, F. Politi, and S. Suga. (2006). "Do Verbs and Adjectives Play Different Roles in Different Cultures? A Cross-Linguistic Analysis of Person Representation." *Journal of Personality and Social Psychology* 90: 734–50.

Maass, A., A. Milesi, S. Zabbini, and D. Stahlberg. (1995). "Linguistic Intergroup Bias: Differential Expectancies or In-Group Protection." *Journal of Personality and Social Psychology* 68: 116–26.

Maass, A., D. Salvi, L. Arcuri, and G. R. Semin. (1989). "Language Use in Intergroup Contexts: The Linguistic Intergroup Bias." *Journal of Personality and Social Psychology* 57: 981–93.

Reitsma-van Rooijen, M., G. R. Semin, and E. van Leeuwen. (2007). "The Effects of Linguistic Abstraction on Interpersonal Distance." *European Journal of Social Psychology* 37: 817–23.

Roszak, J. (2008). "Kulturowe usankcjonowanie alkoholu i przemocy." In R. Szczepanik and J. Wawrzyniak (eds.), *Różne spojrzenia na przemoc*, 167–83. Łódź: Wydawnictwo WSHE.

Rubini, M., and A. W. Kruglanski. (1997). "Brief Encounters Ending in Estrangement: Motivated Language Use and Interpersonal Rapport in the Question-Answer Paradigm." *Journal of Personality and Social Psychology* 72: 1047–60.

Schmid, J. (1999). "Pinning Down Attributions: The Linguistic Category Model Applied to Wrestling Reports." *European Journal of Social Psychology* 29: 895–907.

Schmid, J., K. Fiedler, B. Englich, T. Ehrenberger, and G. R. Semin. (1996). "Taking Sides with the Defendant: Grammatical Choice and the Influence of Implicit Attributions in Prosecutions and Defence Speeches." *International Journal of Psycholinguistics* 12: 127–48.

Semin, G. R. (1995). "Interfacing Language and Social Cognition." *Journal of Language and Social Psychology* 14: 182–94.

Semin, G. (2000). "Agenda 2000: Communication: Language as Implementational Device for Cognition." *European Journal of Social Psychology* 30: 595–612.

Semin, G. R. (2008). "Stereotypes in the Wild." In Y. Kashima, K. Fiedler, and P. Freytag (eds.), *Stereotype Dynamics: Language-Based Approaches to the Formation, Maintenance, and Transformation of Stereotypes*, 11–28. New York: Lawrence Erlbaum Associates.

Semin, G. (2012). "The Linguistic Category Model." In P. A. M. Van Lange, A. Kruglanski, and E. T. Higgins (eds.), *Handbook of Theories of Social Psychology*, Vol. 1, 309–26. Los Angeles: Sage.

Semin, G. R., and K. Fiedler. (1988). "The Cognitive Functions of Linguistic Categories in Describing Persons: Social Cognition and Language." *Journal of Personality and Social Psychology* 54: 558–68.

Semin, G. R., and K. Fiedler. (1989). "Relocating Attributional Phenomena within a Language-Cognition Interface." *European Journal of Social Psychology* 19: 491–508.

Semin, G. R., and K. Fiedler. (1991). "The Linguistic Category Model, Its Bases, Applications and Range." In W. Stroebe and M. Hewstone (eds.), *European Review of Social Psychology*, Vol. 2, 1–30. Chichester: Wiley.

Stangor, C., and M. Schaller. (1996). "Stereotypes as Individual and Collective Stereotypes." In C. N. Macrae, C. Stangor, and M. Hewstone (eds.), *Stereotypes and Stereotyping*, 3–37. New York: Guilford Press.

Webster, D. M., A. W. Kruglanski, and D. A. Pattison. (1997). "Motivated Language Use in Intergroup Contexts: Need-for-Closure Effect on the Linguistic Intergroup Bias." *Journal of Personality and Social Psychology* 72: 490–509.

Wigboldus, D., and K. Douglas. (2007). "Language, Stereotypes, and Intergroup Relations." In K. Fiedler (ed.), *Social Communication*, 79–106. New York: Psychology Press.

Wigboldus, D. H., G. R. Semin, and R. Spears. (2006). "Communicating Expectancies about Others." *European Journal of Social Psychology* 36: 815–24.

6

A Matter of Mental Health?

Treatment of Perpetrators of Domestic Violence in Denmark and the Underlying Perception of Violence

Bo Wagner Sørensen, Denmark

Introduction

This chapter deals with the largest and most well-known treatment program for violent men in contemporary Denmark from an anthropological perspective.[1] Its main purpose is to look into the word *treatment* and how it shapes our understanding of both the violent men and the phenomenon of domestic violence. In other words, what is seen as the problem in need of solution? How is the problem represented (Bacchi 1999; 2009)? In this chapter I am going to highlight and analyze the importance of words and their usage in reference to Danish discourses on treatment programs for abusive men.

The word *treatment* suggests that perpetrators of domestic violence are believed to have some mental illness and/or to have some personality defects. At the same time, treatment programs in Denmark stress—in line with feminist scholars and activists within the field—that perpetrators of domestic violence should take personal responsibility for their violence. This discrepancy between the idea of personal responsibility and the widespread idea of perpetrators of violence being ill is part of the reality of treatment programs. While the therapists subscribe to demands that result from feminist research and activism, their practice often takes on a different course.

Domestic violence has been subject to a growing medicalization that has been quite obvious in recent years. It means that domestic violence is seen as a social health issue rather than a gender issue. One example is that domestic violence and the concept of violence against women have been largely replaced by the gender neutral term *partner violence*, which appears in recent governmental publications. The argument is that a one-sided focus on women as victims of violence takes away a focus on male victimhood. Another common argument is that we have moved beyond a simplistic feminist approach according to which men in general are depicted as enemies and perpetrators. The Danish ideology of gender equality thus materializes in a practice of gender neutrality as regards the phenomenon of domestic violence. The largest treatment program in Denmark, *Dialog mod Vold* (DMV; Dialogue against Violence), and its underlying ideas about the main causes of domestic violence seem to fit in well with this new approach.

The material used for this chapter consists of a variety of sources. My description of DMV is based on material written by the organization itself. Other sources are notes from public presentations and an interview with the director.[2] Apart from these sources of self-presentation, I use external sources, among others a recent evaluation of the treatment programs, which was required by the government.

Country Context: Treatment in Denmark

Specialized treatment directed at men who are violent toward a wife or partner has been available in Denmark for about ten years. Such treatment program offers were part of the Danish government's action plan of March 8, 2002, to combat violence against women. The action plan had four primary foci: support for the victims of violence; activities directed at professionals; procuring/securing knowledge and information about violence; and activities directed at perpetrators of violence (Regeringen 2002: 9–10). The preface to the action plan, signed by the ministers of equality and justice, mentions that "domestic violence must be curtailed. The cycle of violence must be broken by offering treatment to the perpetrator of violence."[3] The government earmarked a substantial sum of money for treatment programs and thus created a market for treatment. Presently, there are four publicly funded treatment programs of varying size: Dialogue against Violence, Alternative to Violence (Roskilde),[4] a treatment program for men at Odense women's shelter,[5] and counseling for men in Herning municipality.[6] In the period of 2009–10, the largest program, Dialogue against Violence, has offered treatment to 442 so-called clients, while the three other programs have offered treatment to between 31 and 40 clients. All programs are free of charge.

These four programs have been evaluated by the National Board of Social Services[7] in order to find out whether treatment of men who perpetrate violence against a wife or a partner result in these men becoming nonviolent (Stevenson et al. 2011: 9). Ultimately, the evaluation is meant to form the basis of an assessment of the future financial support for these treatment programs for violent men. The evaluation concludes that treatment of perpetrators of domestic violence seems to work.[8] At the same time, the evaluators have certain reservations concerning methodology (Stevenson et al. 2011: 180). Most important, the evaluation looks only into the short-term effects of the treatment programs, and even then, the effects are measured primarily according to the perpetrators' and the therapists' views on the results of the programs. The evaluation has tried to integrate how the perpetrator's wife or partner experiences the effects of the treatment programs, but apparently not many wives/partners responded, so the statistical material is limited, and it is very likely that those who responded are more positive than those who did not respond.[9] Another point that is not problematized in the evaluation is that it is hardly any surprise that many men who get a chance of talking about themselves and their emotions during individual and group sessions think that treatment programs make a positive difference in their lives in general. And it is hardly any surprise that the therapists themselves are prone to positive self-evaluation, as their future job and workplace may depend on an evaluation carried out by the National Board of Social Services.

While the evaluation seems to accept the widespread idea, which is also highly present in DMV's therapeutic thinking, that perpetrators of violence need to "get in contact with their emotions" by talking about how they feel, the American consultant on domestic violence, Lundy Bancroft, argues against emotional talk on the part of the perpetrator: "An abuser tries to keep everybody—his partner, his therapist, his friends and relatives— focused on how he feels, so that they won't focus on how he thinks" (Bancroft 2002: 75). Bancroft suggests instead that the perpetrator has to stop focusing on his feelings and his partner's behavior, and look instead at "*her* feelings and *his* behavior" (352). According to Bancroft, therapy typically will not address any of the central causes of abusiveness, including entitlement, coercive control, disrespect, superiority, selfishness, or victim blaming. An abuser program, on the other hand, is expected to cover all these issues and in fact to make them its primary foci (356).

Although the evaluation has its focus on the treatment of *men* who perpetrate violence, its definition of violence is gender neutral—it uses the term *partner violence*—and it is critical of a feminist perspective without providing any substantial critique (Stevenson et al. 2011: 24–25). The nonfeminist and gender-neutral approach that characterizes the evaluation may reflect a concern about objectivity.[10]

Treatment programs have been available for much longer in the other Nordic countries, and they seem to be much more widespread there. ATV (Alternative to Violence) in Norway began in 1987 as a pilot project financed by the Norwegian government. It was the first treatment program in Europe directed at violent men (Stevenson et al. 2011: 55). ATV presents itself as a profeminist program,[11] which is a point that is missed or not considered important in the Danish evaluation of treatment programs. According to a survey of interventions in Sweden, there are fifty public and private organizations dealing with men who are violent, and ten of these organizations were established between the late 1980s and 1996 (Eriksson, Biller, and Balkmar 2006: 6).

Academic Context: On the Concept of Treatment

For years I have been puzzled by the concept of treatment of violent men because of its medical connotations. In Denmark, *treatment*—that is, *behandling* in Danish—is the dominant expression, unlike for instance in the United States and England where concepts such as "programs for men" or "intervention programs" are common (Dobash, Dobash, Cavanagh, and Lewis 2000; Hearn 1998). Programs do not have the medical connotations that treatment has. Sociologist Jeff Hearn writes that men's programs were developed in the late 1970s and early 1980s in the United States as a parallel development to women's refuges and shelters, and that some of the programs were developed in cooperation with women's projects (Hearn 1998: 194). Things have taken another course in the United Kingdom, partly because the women's refuge movement has operated within a policy of minimizing contact with men (ibid.).

Hearn reflects on the idea of "treatment" of men who have been violent, stating that this assumes that it is possible to "treat" this problem. He also points out that the problem of violence appears to be "both *separate from* other parts of the person and at the same time *borne* by the person" (Hearn 1998: 196; orig. italics). Hearn's distinction thus seems to relate to the question of whether it is possible to distinguish between the acts of violence and the man who perpetrates the violence. What is in fact subject to treatment? Is it the acts of violence or the man as such? The notion of "a violent man" suggests that violence is inherent and that "treatment" would imply fundamental changes of personality.

Apparently, treatment, in addition to being offered to patients with medical diseases in the traditional sense, has become the natural solution to any social phenomenon that is seen as unwanted, if not unhealthy, from a Danish societal point of view. Treatment is offered to alcoholics, drug addicts, sex addicts, gambling addicts—to mention the more common "addictions"—and also perpetrators of violence. On the face of it, these phenomena are very different, although some are more different than others. Drug addiction has little in common with perpetration of domestic violence except for the fact that both are subjected to the idea of treatability—or "treatmentality."[12]

In his work on how Danish society deals with drug abuse, anthropologist Steffen Jöhncke (2008) has reflected on treatment, which he describes as a social fact and beyond doubt in policy and practice even though the effects of treatment—that is, treatment as weaning off addiction or ceasing problematic behavior—have never been clearly demonstrated. According to Jöhncke, drug-use treatment—that is, how to go about treating drug users—is a site of political and ideological contestation, but there is a general agreement about the need for treatment as such: "Treatment of drug users [...] is equivalent to the 'help' that is 'offered' to 'other weak groups'—a category to which drug users apparently invariably belong. Treatment is seen as an expression of Danish society, or rather, of the Danish welfare state: The proper thing to do is to help this group of people. More than anything else, the existence of drug use treatment tells about what kind of state and society Danes believe they have or should have" (Jöhncke 2008: 101).

Jöhncke describes how treatment "stands out as an island of decency in a sea of abusive and in other ways unfortunate social relations" (12) and how it holds the promise that drug users may be normalized—that is, weaned off drugs, or in the case of violence, weaned off using violence.

It seems that drug abuse and domestic violence are connected by the common underlying logic of the Danish welfare state. If treatment is presented as the obvious solution to both phenomena, how is the problem understood and represented (Bacchi 1999; 2009)? The answer is that both phenomena are widely thought of as social health problems. The problem of domestic violence thus basically appears to be represented as a social health problem. This medicalization of domestic violence, however, has certain implications, in that it tends to silence sociological and feminist perspectives on domestic violence with likely detrimental effects on women and children, who are the primary victims of domestic violence. When violence is medicalized, it is often degendered and individualized.

Although practical work and research with perpetrators of domestic violence indicate that most offenders regard it as their right to control women, a number of different explanations have developed that do not recognize domestic violence as a gendered problem of power and control (Harne and Radford 2008: 155; see also Merry 2009 on gender violence and entitlements). Different explanations also mean different ways of trying to change violent men. Many of these nonfeminist approaches originated in the United States, which has a longer history of working with perpetrators. The American psychologist David Adams (1990) has described and critiqued these approaches that located the problem as a matter of mental health—as a matter of men in need of treatment (Harne and Redford 2008: 155). According to Harne and Redford,

> By locating the problem of domestic violence in some kind of psychological disorder, psycho-therapeutic approaches often feed into the commonly accepted excuses that perpetrators use to explain their violence. Psychological discourses of dependency or co-dependency, poor ego functioning, low self-esteem, insecurity, unresolved conflicts with parents, and "emotional repression" are amongst numerous psyche discourses which serve to focus the problem away from violent men's responsibility for their violence and the benefits they gain from it.

Empirical Data: Dialogue against Violence

Dialogue against Violence (DMV) started out in Copenhagen in 2002 as provider of a program for perpetrators of domestic violence, a niche created by the government and ensuing public funding.[13] In 2005, the organization expanded with two additional departments in Aarhus and Odense, and in 2008, it launched "the mobile team," which primarily has contact with the municipalities outside the three cities. In 2008, DMV also began to cooperate with the Prison Service in order to offer treatment in connection with serving a prison sentence.[14] DMV's expansion has been legitimated by the need to be a nationwide organization so that perpetrators of domestic violence all over the country can be offered treatment close to their home. At the same time, DMV has argued in favor of taking a broad approach to domestic violence by working not just with the perpetrators of violence but also with their partners and the whole family. According to DMV's website, "Dialogue against Violence is a treatment offered to persons who perpetrate violence in close relations."[15] The choice of the word *persons* is not accidental; DMV also offers special treatment for "women who perpetrate partner violence" (Stevenson et al. 2011: 170). DMV's website also notes that the perpetrator's partner is offered parallel individual counseling and therapy, while the children, as part of a special project that began in 2009, can have individual therapy and group sessions parallel with their parents' treatment. DMV's expansion has been made possible by public funding that has increased over the years.

DMV has been marketing itself by trying to appeal to common sense. The organization's self-presentation goes like this (Hensen and Petersen 2004): The traditional way of combating violence against women has been to focus on the woman, the victim of violence, and use the resources to help and protect *her*. Another way, the new way, is to focus on the man, the perpetrator of violence, because he is responsible for the violence. It stares you in the face that in order to stop the violence, efforts should be concentrated on offering help and treatment to the perpetrator and making a permanent change of attitude in him. Only then will the violence not be repeated in new relationships or passed on to the children.

From the very start, DMV has promoted the idea of violence as social heredity.[16] People grow up in violent families and repeat the pattern of violence when they get older and have families of their own because they have never learned other ways, and they have never had the "tools" to break the cycle of violence. Violence is the "language" they turn to in conflicts because it is the only language they know. DMV very soon produced figures that showed that 98.2 percent of perpetrators of violence had experienced violence in their early childhood (Hensen and Petersen 2004: 22). These figures were based on what they refer to as their own research, which means that they are based on their clients' reports. Figures are powerful and tend to assume a life of their own,[17] even when they are of dubious validity. There are no methodological reflections in Per Hensen and Helle Peterson's book on what it means to "have experienced violence in one's early childhood" or if some of the clients would have been tempted to tick the box and/or say yes in any case. It is common knowledge that people who can claim they had an abusive childhood will be partly excused and have diminished responsibility for their violence in their adult life. It is also well known that organizations such as DMV tend to overestimate the link between childhood experience and adult behavior, because they only count men with violent childhoods who are violent but not men with violent childhoods who are not violent. DMV is unlikely to ever have contact with this latter group of men.[18]

In any case, the figures are part of DMV's claim to legitimacy: "[T]he social heredity is a decisive factor in the circle [cycle] of violence that needs to be broken by offering treatment to men who perpetrate violence" (ibid.). DMV entered the field with an offer that was almost too good to resist. The organization claimed that they could nip violence in the bud by breaking the vicious intergenerational cycle of violence. They would go directly for the perceived root causes of violence instead of just providing patch-up solutions. They argued that if you work with male perpetrators and offer them treatment, you end up treating entire families and getting closer to the ultimate goal of a healthy society.[19]

With their focus on perpetrators, DMV presented themselves to the public, not least the politicians, as an alternative to other agents in the field of domestic violence because of their new approach. The director—then head—of DMV often appeared in the media, where she advertised the organization's treatment work and the basic thoughts about breaking the vicious cycle of violence. And the organization was not only presented as an alternative as regards the approach; it was also presented as professional and evidence based.[20]

In 2005, the director of DMV was interviewed by the editor of a magazine published by Dansk Kvindesamfund, the oldest women's organization in Denmark (Deleuran 2005a, 2005b). One of the articles opens with a summary of the director's critical remarks about the women's movement and the shelter movement, both of which have failed in their efforts to deal with domestic violence and help the victims of violence. The director goes on to say that she is not impressed with the results these movements have produced during the 25 years they have had center stage. In her view, part of the problem is that they have held too rigid an attitude toward men and have not been willing to cooperate outside their own narrow circles. This has bungled the common goal of helping violent families. And she concludes that the women's movement and the shelter movement have not been professional enough (Deleuran 2005b). The director and DMV have later tried to patch up the relationship with the shelters and LOKK, the national organization of shelters, and now there is some cooperation between the parties.

In the public self-representation of DMV, the organization is in big demand. It seems there are always people on the waiting list,[21] which is used as a signal to politicians to put more money into treatment. From the day of the opening in August 2002, several men made applications or inquiries: "Men who had carried their shame and guilt of beating the one they love, and who finally saw a possibility to get help," as DMV puts it (Hensen and Petersen 2004: 13).

DMV's director often presents the issue of domestic violence in the way of a question when she is out in the public: How cool do you think it is for a man to sometimes have to hit the woman he loves? Chapter 1 in DMV's book, in which they present themselves and their work, is called "Why hit the one you love?" (Hensen and Petersen 2004: 17). By foregrounding love and the apparent paradox of using violence against the person you love, the scene is set for a psychological discourse. The emphasis on love may come as no surprise, since it is a convention among the Danish majority population that intimate relationships and marriages are based on love. Love, however, is a broad category and a slippery term with many meanings. The focus on "the man who loves" may also be seen as part of DMV's politics that the perpetrator should be met with respect and dialogue, because, as DMV puts it, "there is a crisis-ridden man behind every battered woman" (Hensen and Petersen 2004: 17). According to DMV, the men's violence is part of an ingrained or deep-rooted pattern, which makes it impossible for the men to stop or change on their own, even if they want it badly. This is not confirmed by my own empirical data from three major studies of domestic violence, according to which men are usually in control of their violence.[22] They act when they believe the situation calls for it. And often they are not violent until the relationship is relatively secure and they have obtained a "license to beat," which means that violence is not really an impulsive and uncontrolled act.

The men who make use of DMV are first described as very diverse, representing different social classes (Hensen and Petersen 2004: 19). Later, however, it appears that DMV's target group can be categorized into two main personality types.[23] One is the person who acts out, has antisocial traits, and acts on impulse when he comes across problems. The other is the passive-aggressive person who tends to control his surroundings because of a strong inner insecurity (25f.). How these psychiatric diagnoses of perpetrators of domestic violence combine with the idea of the vicious cycle of violence is not clear. Another thing is that the focus on personality type means that violence is given little attention. Violence is seen as a mere symptom of personality type. The act of violence tends to disappear in this perspective, and when the act of violence disappears so does the victim of violence. Considering that the perpetrator's violence against his wife or partner used to be the main issue and the very reason he entered the treatment program in the first place, it is interesting that it tends to disappear while the individual man's personality moves center stage.

DMV presents the following definition of domestic violence: Systematic use of violence and abuse to gain power over and control of a partner or ex-partner (Hensen and Petersen 2004: 21). However, this aspect of power disappears in the rest of the 160 pages of the book and is not integrated into any thinking behind the treatment program.[24]

The concept of treatment is not questioned in the books published by DMV staff; treatment is taken as a matter of fact. DMV's ultimate goal is to stop the violence. To reach that goal, the client has to go through a number of processes, which involve taking responsibility for his violence, coming to terms with his own violent past and painful childhood experiences, learning new ways of communicating, trying out new experiences, and always having a focus on his inner dialogues and feelings of powerlessness (Hensen and Petersen 2004: 24f.). The issue of gender entitlements, which is key to profeminist men's programs, is not mentioned by DMV, and neither are the aspects of power and control. Instead, powerlessness is emphasized.[25]

The program is divided into different phases: individual therapeutic sessions; group sessions; integration/individual sessions; discharge/individual sessions (32). A full treatment takes one to one-and-a-half years depending on the client. Since DMV started, 708 men and women have been offered treatment (Stevenson et al. 2011: 63). DMV's therapeutic work is based on cognitive and psychodynamic theory and different techniques of self, such as mindfulness and narrative therapy (Hensen and Petersen 2004; Stevenson et al. 2011: 67).[26]

A careful reading of the treatment offered by DMV does not bring much clarity to a person who has a gendered perspective on domestic violence and who is not familiar with therapy. It remains a "black box" much like one Jöhncke talks about in his book on treatment for drug abusers (Jöhncke 2008). And according to his experience, the black box is empty: "What I have argued is that […] the black box is empty, the idea of treatment as something *real* is an effect only of particular ways of thinking, talking and handling it" (Jöhncke 2008: 44). Initially, he, too, wanted to find out what treatment was about: "[I]t took me some time to realise fully that the object I was trying to understand—but that always seemed to remain just outside my grasp—was constituted by treatment in this sense of an on-going construction of political and institutional meaning. For a while, I kept looking for where 'the treatment'—the actual thing—was, *where* it was happening *within* all the activities that I was witnessing. Perhaps one day I could be lucky enough to understand exactly what staff referred to, when they said that they were 'doing treatment'" (Jöhncke 2008: 35). Jöhncke goes on to say that eventually he realized that treatment ceases to make sense as an essence, a hidden and inherent effect, when it is held up to scrutiny: What there is to study are practices that are given the label "treatment."

Empirical Data: A Social Health Problem

In June 2010 the Danish government launched the so-called *National Strategy to Combat Intimate Partner Violence*.[27] This strategy was a follow-up on two preceding action plans from 2002 and 2005. The first one, titled *The Government's Action Plan to Combat Violence against Women*, was published on International Women's Day, March 8; the second one had a somewhat similar title: *Action Plan to Combat Men's Violence against Women and Children in the Family 2005–2008*.[28] It appears from the titles that there has been a shift from a focus on men's violence against women and children in the first two action plans to a focus on intimate partner violence in the last one. This shift is not accidental.[29] The national strategy avoids using the concept of violence against women altogether, while at the same time the meaning of gender is downplayed. Neither does the strategy speak of gender-based violence, gender violence, or domestic violence as a human rights issue, although these terms are standard in international organizations such as the World Health Organization and the United Nations (Youngs 2003; Kelly 2005; Merry 2009). The national strategy uses the term *partner violence* instead.

In the preface to the national strategy, violence is presented as a natural force—or medical disease—that strikes people: "Still every year around 28,000 women and 9,000 men are hit by partner violence" (Regeringen 2010: 5).[30] And it is stressed that prevention should have top priority. Treatment of perpetrators is also mentioned, and it appears that "many perpetrators wish to stop the violence but are not able to do it on their own" (12).

Other initiatives point in the same gender-neutral direction. One example is a discussion paper called *Ud af familiens vold* (*Ways out of Family Violence*) that was developed by the independent think tank Mandag Morgen in cooperation with TrygFonden.[31] The discussion paper, which was prepared with the explicit aim of influencing the political agenda, was combined with a big conference in 2011 where all actors in the field—that is, shelter staff, social workers, researchers, and not least politicians—were invited. The basic message was that we need new thinking, a professionalization in the field, and a targeted prevention directed at the groups where violence is more prevalent. Interestingly, these points are very close to the Danish government's national strategy on "partner violence." New thinking, according to the discussion paper, means that we have to break with the tendency so far to only think of women as victims of violence: "The approach to violence has become much more nuanced. Partner violence is no longer seen as something that strikes women [only]. This is why you do not just talk about 'violence against women,' but about 'violence in close relationships' or 'partner violence.' Since the 1990s it has become widely accepted that the violent men also need support and treatment. [. . .] Today there are offers of treatment for the violent men [. . .] But there are still no offers of support or treatment for men who are victims of violence" (Mandag Morgen and TrygFonden 2011: 22; my translation). The discussion paper also comments on the historic link between the women's movement and the field of violence against women, but with the twist that this link is seen as a likely hindrance to developing the work against violence, because a gender-political approach is seen as acting against an evidence-based approach that offers insight into the true nature of violence, its prevalence, and it prevention.[32] This leads to the following recommendation of a new approach in the field:

> Violence in close relationships should be treated to a larger degree as a social problem and less as a gender equality and gender politics issue. The gender equality perspective has been a major issue in the work [...] and it is also a major issue in the prevention work, where dissemination of gender equality is an important element. But the gender political rhetoric that characterises the field to some extent can be a hindrance to develop and introduce light and shade into the work against violence. If violence in close relationships is regarded as a particular gender political problem instead of a social problem, it curbs the possibilities for the exchange of knowledge and learning from other fields dealing with social and social health politics. There is a risk that the gender political perspective hinders that the field gets expanded with new parties who could contribute to raise [the level of] the work—that the field closes in around itself. On top of that there is a risk that the gender political rhetoric leads to a debate without any nuances where it becomes a matter of "men against women." (Mandag Morgen and TrygFonden 2011: 14; my translation)

In late November 2009 the conference *How All Men Can Help—When Some Men Are Perpetrators of Violence* took place in Copenhagen. It was a conference for men only, arranged by the National Board of Social Services, the National Organisation of Shelters, and Dialogue against Violence. The keynote speaker was the American educator and social theorist Jackson Katz, who is the founder of Mentors in Violence Prevention.[33] The purpose of the conference was to engage more ordinary men in the work against domestic violence and make them take responsibility and become mentors or role models for other men in different fields and work places. A network of men was formed as a follow-up to the conference.[34] In late 2011 the network sent out a summary of a meeting in which it had been decided to regard the perpetrator of domestic violence as a person who had a problem and consequently should be offered treatment. The network had also talked about establishing a targeted campaign that made use of new and different ways of representing the perpetrator of violence. The idea was to show pictures of a crying man in order to show that the perpetrator of violence is also a victim.[35] Treatment has entered the field of domestic violence in Denmark and it is likely to stay.

Analysis and Discussion: Treatment and Perspectives on Domestic Violence

If I raise any critique of treatment of perpetrators of violence, people usually respond, "Do you suggest that we should do *nothing*?" It is as if people in general see treatment as the only solution to the problem. Who can argue against treatment if treatment is considered *the* solution? Treatment seems to send a message that we, the society, care about our fellow citizens and allow them back if they are prepared to change for the better. And most people think that perpetrators of violence are prepared to change their ways because it does not really do them any good to be violent. Violence is generally seen as a symptom of underlying problems, and not just any problems, but problems that go deep. This perspective is part of the reason we are reminded that men are victims, too: not just victims of (partner) violence, but victims of childhood experiences, nagging wives, and societal stress. The following anecdote illustrates the absurdity of this perspective: At an EU conference on gender violence many years ago, a Danish medical doctor gave a paper on the stressful lives of men and the many demands they have to meet.[36] In conclusion she said, "It is with men as it is with dogs. If you tease them enough, they will bite." She therefore suggested that we should all be nicer and more considerate toward men.[37]

Treatment is a problematic concept when it is combined with violence, because it evokes a medicalized discourse according to which the perpetration of violence is a mere reaction to circumstances beyond the perpetrator's control. There are two main theoretical perspectives on violence (Sørensen 2005; 2008). According to one perspective, some men are violent because they can.[38] According to the other perspective, they are violent because they cannot help it. The first perspective is based in sociological, anthropological, and feminist theory, whereas the other perspective is based in psychiatry, individual psychology, and psychotherapy. Interestingly, many people are offended by the statement "because they can," as the underlying perspective on violence is seen as cynical, arrogant, immoral, and superficial. Many people are drawn to what they believe to be deep explanations, and deep explanations tend to go back in time and involve people's childhood experiences.[39]

"Because they can" is firmly grounded in basic ideas about the interrelationship between gender, power, and control. Violence is perpetrated, as a general rule, by the more powerful to control and discipline the less powerful. Domestic violence can be seen as the ultimate form of categorization (Jenkins 1997: 106); the victim of violence is put in her (right) place according to cultural ideas about gender orders (Lundgren 1990; 1993). Another important aspect is that, from the perpetrator's point of view, violence works (Riches 1986; Ptacek 1990; Bancroft 2002). Some people working in the domestic violence treatment industry are very aware of that. Lundy Bancroft is a case in point: "I regret to say that a majority of abusers choose not to do the work. It isn't that they *can't* change [. . .] but that they decide they don't wish to. They run a sort of cost-benefit analysis in their heads and decide that the rewards of remaining in control of their partners outweigh the costs. [. . .] everything having to do with relationships and the particular women they are with" (Bancroft 2002: 357).

"Because they cannot help it" is a health-oriented perspective inspired by a mix of psychotherapeutic and socialization theories that tend to locate the root cause of violence in the psyche of the individual person (man), whose wife or partner can trigger his violence by pushing—with or without intent—the right buttons. The combined aspects of gender and power are considered to be of little importance in this perspective. Instead, powerlessness, feeling powerless, and low self-esteem are key words that sum up what is believed to characterize the typical perpetrator, besides whatever "diagnoses" he may have. It is usually believed that those feelings and thoughts—or perhaps rather, those deep-seated, unhealthy psychological patterns—have been instilled in the person during childhood.

The two perspectives invite different prevention strategies.[40] "Because they can" points in the direction of making it harder for the men to *practice* their violence by creating a climate of zero tolerance in the community and society. This also means that people in general should abstain from tendencies to blame the victim and excuse the perpetrator on whatever grounds: "Almost anyone can become an ally of an abusive man by inadvertently adopting his perspective" (Bancroft 2002: 288). Gender politics and a consistent terminology are both highly relevant for this prevention strategy. "Because they cannot help it," on the other hand, is a perspective that seems to invite a more narrow prevention strategy. The prime target is the perpetrator, who should be offered and receive treatment, after which he can come out as a new man weaned off violence. Interestingly, perhaps as part of the current focus on treatment in Denmark, a man came out in public as a former perpetrator of domestic violence who had been weaned off violence by one of the treatment programs, Alternative to Violence.[41] His story was highlighted as a real success story, he was invited to join the men's network, and many people in the field used him as an example to argue that treatment works. DMV followed up on that at their ten-year jubilee in 2012, where the invited guests could meet three clients, one former and two actual, who would tell their stories of treatment and becoming weaned off violence.

Conclusion

Does it make sense to claim, as DMV does, that the perpetrator of domestic violence is responsible for his violence, when the same program seems to operate with the idea that the perpetrator of violence is mentally ill or has some kind of personality disorder or defect in addition to not being able to stop his violence without professional help? It seems there is a mismatch between underlying logics. The demand on the perpetrator to take responsibility seems to be the merit of the women's movement. Initially, this demand was radical. Eventually, however, it became mainstream. Currently, it is a mindless convention and sometimes an empty phrase. The answer to the question is that it does not make sense—that he cannot be held responsible or only partly responsible. And "partly responsible" is in line with "also a victim," which may in fact be closer to DMV's treatment practice. Public speeches or presentations by staff have revealed that (at least some) staff perceive domestic violence as a relational problem and a problem of poor communication skills on both sides.[42] It is likely that these perceptions will influence staff members' therapeutic work with perpetrators of domestic violence.

I think Jöhncke has a point when he comments on "the obviousness of treatment" and says, "However problematic drug use treatment may be . . . we cannot *not* have it" (Jöhncke 2008: 45). The Danish welfare state is supposed to offer treatment to people who are supposed to be in need of treatment—who need to be normalized. Treatment is a seductive term;

it invokes images of curing and healing, and it places domestic violence squarely within a social health framework. What is worrying, though, is that a gendered phenomenon like domestic violence becomes degendered and depowered in the process and ends up being represented as an individualized matter of social and mental health. This skewing of the phenomenon is not just a matter of words—just words—if by that we mean that it does not really matter what things are called. Words matter; words are powerful because they assist in shaping our social reality. *Treatment* is one such word that, at least in Denmark, seems to frame our perception of domestic violence, which by implication becomes subject to treatability. When a gendered phenomenon is recategorized and transformed into a social health problem, it has serious implications, not least for the victims of domestic violence.

References

Adams, David. (1990). "Treatment Models of Men Who Batter: A Profeminist Analysis." In Kersti Yllö and Michele Bograd (eds.), *Feminist Perspectives on Wife Abuse*, 176–99. Newbury Park: Sage.

Bacchi, Carol. (1999). *Women, Policy and Politics: The Construction of Policy Problems*. London: Sage.

Bacchi, Carol. (2009). *Analysing Policy: What's the Problem Represented to Be?* French's Forest, NSW: Pearson Education.

Bancroft, Lundy. (2002). *Why Does He Do That? Inside the Minds of Angry and Controlling Men*. New York: G. P. Putnam's Sons.

Danneskiold-Samsøe, Sofie, Yvonne Mørck, and Bo Wagner Sørensen. (2011). *"Familien betyder alt": Vold mod kvinder i etniske minoritetsfamilier*. Frederiksberg: Frydenlund.

Deleuran, Jane. (2005a). "Voldelige mænd stiller krav." *Kvinden & Samfundet* 121 (1): 6–7.

Deleuran, Jane. (2005b). "Kvindebevægelsen svigtede voldsramte kvinder." *Kvinden & Samfundet* 121 (1): 8.

Dobash, Rebecca Emerson, Russell P. Dobash, Kate Cavanagh, and Ruth Lewis. (2000). *Changing Violent Men*. Thousand Oaks: Sage.

Ejrnæs, Morten, Gorm Gabrielsen, and Per Nørrung, eds. (2004). *Social opdrift—social arv*. Copenhagen: Akademisk Forlag.

Eriksson, Maria, Helene Biller, and Dag Balkmar. (2006). *Mäns våldsutövande—barns upplevelser: En kartläggning av interventioner, kunskap och utvecklingsbehov.* Stockholm: Näringsdepartementet, Regeringskansliet and Fritzes.

Gelles, Richard J. (1997). *Intimate Violence in Families.* Thousand Oaks: Sage.

Grønvald Raun, Katrine (2010). "Voldelige mænd ender på venteliste." *Nationalt,* July 23, 2010. Accessed June 10, 2013. http://www.b.dk/danmark/voldelige-maend-ender-paa-venteliste.

Harne, Lynne, and Jill Radford. (2010[2008]). *Tackling Domestic Violence: Theories, Policies and Practice.* Maidenhead, Berkshire: McGraw Hill, Open University Press.

Hearn, Jeff. (1998). *The Violences of Men.* London: Sage.

Hensen, Per I. (2007). *Vold i familien i Danmark: Beskrivelse af de voldelige mænd, som har deltaget i det danske behandlingsprogram "Dialog mod Vold."* Copenhagen: Askovgården.

Hensen, Per I., and Helle Øbo Petersen. (2004). *Dialog mod Vold.* Århus: Systime Academic.

Isdal, Per. (2000). *Meningen med volden.* Oslo: Kommuneforlaget.

Jenkins, Richard. (1997). *Rethinking Ethnicity: Arguments and Explorations.* London: Sage.

Johansson, Paul. (2010). *Behandlingsforskning—utøvere av vold mot partner: Oversikt over forskning på feltet.* Oslo: Nasjonalt kunnskapssenter om vold og traumatisk stress (NKVTS).

Jöhncke, Steffen. (2008). *Treatment Trouble: On the Politics of Methadone and Anthropology.* PhDDissertation, Institute of Anthropology, University of Copenhagen.

Kelly, Liz. (2005). "Inside Outsiders: Mainstreaming Violence against Women into Human Rights Discourse and Practice." *International Feminist Journal of Politics* 7 (4): 471–95.

Lundgren, Eva. (1990). *Gud og hver mann: Seksualisert vold som kulturell arena for å skape kjønn.* Oslo: Cappelen.

Lundgren, Eva. (1993). *Det får da være grenser for kjønn: Voldelig empiri og feministisk teori.* Oslo: Universitetsforlaget

Mandag Morgen and TrygFonden. (2011). *Ud af familiens vold: Debat om indsatsen mod vold i nære relationer.* Copenhagen: Mandag Morgen and TrygFonden.

Merry, Sally Engle. (2009). *Gender Violence: A Cultural Perspective.* Malden, MA: WileyBlackwell.

Mørck, Yvonne, Bo Wagner Sørensen, Sofie Danneskiold-Samsøe, and Henriette Højberg. (2011). "The Thin Line between Protection, Care and Control: Violence against Ethnic Minority Women in Denmark." In Ravi K. Thiara, Stéphanie A. Condon, and Monika Schröttle (eds.), *Violence against Women and Ethnicity: Commonalities and Differences across Europe*, 276–90. Opladen: Barbara Budrich Publishers.

Ptacek, James. (1990). "Why Do Men Batter Their Wives?" In Kersti Yllö and Michele Bograd (eds.), *Feminist Perspectives on Wife Abuse*, 133–57. London: Sage.

Råkil, Marius, ed. (2002). *Menns vold mot kvinner—behandlingserfaringer og kunnskapsstatus*. Oslo: Universitetsforlaget.

Regeringen. (2002). *Regeringens handlingsplan til bekæmpelse af vold mod kvinder*. Copenhagen.

Regeringen. (2005). *Handlingsplan til bekæmpelse af mænds vold mod kvinder og børn i familien 2005–2008*. Copenhagen.

Regeringen. (2010). *National strategi til bekæmpelse af vold i nære relationer*. Copenhagen.

Riches, David. (1986). "The Phenomenon of Violence." In David Riches (ed.), *The Anthropology of Violence*, 1–27. Oxford: Blackwell.

Sørensen, Bo Wagner. (1990). "Folk Models of Wife-Beating in Nuuk, Greenland." *Folk, Journal of the Danish Ethnographic Society* 32: 93–115.

Sørensen, Bo Wagner. (1994). *Magt eller afmagt? Køn, følelser og vold i Grønland*. Copenhagen: Akademisk Forlag.

Sørensen, Bo Wagner. (1998). "Explanations for Wife Beating in Greenland." In Renate C. A. Klein (ed.), *Multidisciplinary Perspectives on Family Violence*, 153–75. London: Routledge.

Sørensen, Bo Wagner. (2001). "'Men in Transition': The Representation of Men's Violence against Women in Greenland." *Violence Against Women* 7 (7): 826–47.

Sørensen, Bo Wagner. (2005). "Different Understandings of Violence against Women and Their Implications." Paper presented at the 2nd Sino-Nordic Women and Gender Studies Conference, "Gender and Human Rights in China and the Nordic Countries," Malmö, Sweden, August 7–9.

Sørensen, Bo Wagner. (2008). "De kan sagtens la' være." *Weekendavisen* no. 15, April 11.

Sørensen, Bo Wagner, Yvonne Mørck, and Sofie Danneskiold-Samsøe. (2012a). "A Conspiracy of Silence: Violence against Ethnic Minority Women in Denmark." In Barbro Wijma, Claire Tucker, and Ulrica Engdahl (eds.), *GEXcel Work in Progress Report Volume XIII. Proceedings from the Conference: Violences and Silences: Shaming, Blaming—and Intervening*, 133–38. October 12–14, 2010, Linköping University, Linköping, Sweden. Linköping: Centre of Gender Excellence—GEXcel.

Sørensen, Bo Wagner, Yvonne Mørck, and Sofie Danneskiold-Samsøe. (2012b). "Tavshed og vold mod kvinder: Erfaringer fra et projekt om vold mod kvinder i etniske minoritetsfamilier." *Tidsskriftet Antropologi* 65: 103–27.

Stevenson, Gráinne, Kirstina Stenager, and Lise Barlach. (2011). *Behandling af mænd der udøver vold: Evaluering af fire projekter*. Odense: Servicestyrelsen.

Youngs, Gillian. (2003). "Private Pain/Public Peace: Women's Rights as Human Rights and Amnesty International's Report on Violence against Women." *Signs* 28 (4): 1209–29.

Notes

1. I use the term *treatment program* because this is widely used in the specialist literature in English. The common term used in Denmark is *behandlingstilbud*, which translates as "treatment offer" or "offer of treatment."

2. The interview took place in April 2010. It was done in cooperation with Yvonne Mørck and Sofie Danneskiold-Samsøe as part of a project on violence against ethnic minority women in Denmark. See Danneskiold-Samsøe, Mørck, and Sørensen (2011); Mørck et al. (2011); Sørensen, Mørck, and Danneskiold-Samsøe (2012a, 2012b).

3. This is my translation from the original Danish: "Volden i hjemmet skal bremses. Voldscirklen skal brydes ved behandling af voldsudøveren." *Vold i hjemmet* translates into *domestic violence* and is used indiscriminately with *vold i familien*—that is, *violence in the family*. They are the most common expressions in Denmark. People inspired by feminist thinking on the subject, however, prefer *violence against women*, even though the term *partner violence* is getting widespread even among shelter workers. Mainly specialists use the term *gender-based violence*.

4. *Alternativ til Vold* in Danish, often abbreviated to ATV. It is based on the teachings of ATV in Norway. Roskilde is a town located south of Copenhagen.

5. *Krisecenter Odenses behandlingstilbud til mænd* in Danish.

6. *Manderådgivningen i Herning Kommune* in Danish. Herning is a town in Jutland.

7. The National Board of Social Services—*Servicestyrelsen* in Danish—is an independent subdivision of the Ministry of Social Affairs and Integration. According to the website, "The Danish Parliament decides the political, social and welfare initiatives to be implemented in Denmark. The National Board of Social Services is charged with ensuring that such initiatives are put into practice in Denmark's local authorities as intended by the Parliament and to counsel and assist local authorities."

8. A survey of research on treatment of perpetrators of violence against partners published by the Norwegian Centre for Violence and Traumatic Stress Studies concludes that little or no effect can be demonstrated on the basis of specific interventions (Johansson 2010).

9. According to the evaluation, the number of perpetrators' wives/partners is unknown (Stevenson et al.2011: 94). This point is telling considering that the issue is domestic violence and whether or not domestic violence treatment programs work.

10. The evaluation, however, brings a citation by one of the clients in the colophon. His argument is that he lacked tools for solving conflicts with his wife and children until he entered a treatment program, and that he was not equipped with these tools by his own parents. It is likely that the authors share such a perspective on domestic violence based on the cycle of violence and poor communication skills, since it is highlighted and not questioned.

11. See ATV-Roskilde's homepage about the organization's basic conception of violence: http://www.alternativtilvold.dk/voldsopfattelser .asp. The work of one of the founders of ATV especially is widespread in Denmark. See Isdal (2000); see also Råkil (2002). In spite of possible differences between the treatment organizations, ATV refers clients to DMV.

12. See Jöhncke (2008: 103f.).

13. See their website: http://www.dialogmodvold.dk.

14. According to DMV, this cooperation project has not been very successful so far, in that not many inmates have been in treatment. It is not clear, however, if it is due to the inmates' or the Prison Service's lack of interest.
15. In Danish: "Dialog mod Vold er et behandlingstilbud tilpersoner, der udøver vold i nære relationer."
16. The concept of negative social heredity is widespread in Denmark and the other Scandinavian countries. It was introduced in the late 1960s and has become common property, which means that both ordinary people and politicians can relate to it. Some Danish sociologists have argued that it should be abandoned as a scientific concept due to its lack of precision (Ejrnæs et al. 2004).
17. The (revised) figures appear on the front page of the National Organisation of Shelters website in March 2012. The text, which appears as a facts box, reads, "According to Dialogue against Violence 80 percent of the perpetrators of violence have experienced violence in the family when they were kids." See http://www.lokk.dk.
18. Thanks to Renate Klein for providing this important point.
19. This argument is the reverse of the argument that is commonly used in development aid: To invest in women is to invest in entire families and ultimately communities.
20. The two books published by DMV—Hensen and Petersen (2004) and Hensen (2007)—present themselves as research. The evaluation on treatment programs in Denmark comments on the latter, saying that it is unclear and not thoroughly prepared (Stevenson et al. 2011: 173).
21. The many men who are on a waiting list seems to be a constant theme when the director of DMV is interviewed by the media. In an interview in 2010, she says, "It is deeply shameful that we have men on our waiting list in both Copenhagen and Aarhus. Men that we know are violent against their partners. This is critical." (Grønvald Raun 2010).
22. The first study was based on fieldwork in Nuuk, Greenland, in 1988–89. See Sørensen (1990, 1994, 1998, 2001). The second interview-based study was carried out in 2009–10 with two colleagues. Its focus was ethnic minority women in Denmark. See Danneskiold-Samsøe, Mørck, and Sørensen (2011); Mørck et al. (2011); Sørensen, Mørck, and Danneskiold-Samsøe (2012a, 2012b). The third study titled "Stories and Understandings of Violence" (in Danish: "Voldsfortællinger og voldsforståelser") is ongoing and

financed by the Danish Council for Independent Research / Social Sciences (FSE). It is interview-based with a focus on Danish majority women. This chapter was written as part of the project.

23. Clients are screened and subsequently given a psychological profile in order for the treatment institution to have the best possible knowledge about "the violent man's characteristics" (Hensen and Petersen 2004: 103).

24. The many inconsistencies may partly be explained by the two authors' different backgrounds. One, the woman director, is a pedagogue, whereas the other is a male psychologist with a psychiatric background, which stands out clearly in the book and the references.

25. Apparently DMV does not follow the guidelines for programs working with male perpetrators of domestic violence developed by researchers and activists in the EU: http://www.work-with-perpetrators.eu. The director has publicly stated on several occasions that domestic violence and, consequently, DMV's work is not a gender issue and even that it has nothing to do with gender. One occasion was during a panel debate arranged by LOKK: "Men's Violence—Women's Fight?!" ("Mænds vold—kvinders kamp?!"), Copenhagen, June 8, 2011.

26. See also DMV's website: http://www.dialogmodvold.dk/Behandling/Teori/tabid/2150/Default.aspx.

27. "National strategi til bekæmpelse af vold i nære relationer" in Danish.

28. "Regeringens handlingsplan til bekæmpelse af vold mod kvinder" and "Handlingsplan til bekæmpelse af mænds vold mod kvinder og børn i familien 2005–2008" in Danish. See Regeringen (2002, 2005).

29. It has been confirmed at a public meeting by one of the staff in the Gender Equality Department, who was happy about the toning down of old-fashioned and simplistic feminist perspectives as he saw it.

30. Prevalence studies on men's violence against women in Denmark have been published in 2004 and 2007 by the National Institute of Public Health. The institute also published a prevalence study of violence against men in 2008.

31. Mandag Morgen was established in 1989. According to their website, their job is "to enable key decision makers to navigate and operate in an increasingly fragmented and complex society. This calls for new shared understandings and solutions" (http://www.mm.dk). Tryg-Fonden is a private foundation. It supports projects that contribute to an increased sense of safety locally and nationally.

32. DMV was represented in the reference group.

33. See his website: http://www.jacksonkatz.com/mvp.html.

34. The members have been few and the network has been about to close down more than once before it finally closed down in mid-2012. A substantial part of the members were therapists. The main concern of some of them was not the victims of domestic violence but rather that male perpetrators of violence are sometimes stigmatized and demonized in public. The focus of the network was "working with men," but some of Katz's basic points seem to have been lost.

35. *Victim* was put in quotation marks in the original text.

36. Her focus was health oriented, and she pointed out men's shorter life expectancy compared to women, and so on. Men's health studies represent a field that is often not really aware of the meaning of gender in spite of its focus on men.

37. The female speaker was absolutely serious about it. The startled audience, however, most of whom were women, did not know how to react. Some began to laugh; some said "woof."

38. Gelles (1997: 133) writes that family members are (sometimes) violent because they *can*.

39. See also Sørensen (1990, 1994, 1998, 2001) on explanations for domestic violence in Nuuk, Greenland.

40. See Danneskiold-Samsøe, Mørck, and Sørensen (2011: 39ff.).

41. He appeared in several papers, and treatment institution staff were interviewed at the same time. The 45-year-old man had been a client of ATV for three years. See http://www.alternativtilvold.dk/filer/roskildedagbladmarts2010.pdf; http://www.alternativtilvold.dk/filer/flemmingijp.pdf.

42. Both ideas are widespread in the Danish population, including therapists. I refer to a presentation by psychologist Jacob Fogh, DMV, at a dialogue meeting titled "Violence against Women!" organized by FIU-Ligestilling, Copenhagen, November 25, 2011, and another public presentation by psychologist Helle Hundahl, DMV, at a debate meeting on men, divorce, and violence held by Mandecentret, Copenhagen, November 6, 2012. When Hundahl mentioned the personal responsibility of the perpetrator of violence, her statement was followed by a "but," and she ended up saying that it takes two and that women should be more aware about the tone they use in arguments.

7

Dangerous Words

How Euphemisms May Imperil Women's Lives

Britta Mogensen, Denmark

Introduction

Immigration from third-world countries into Denmark for the past thirty to forty years has challenged our way of life and allowed for a look into other cultures and traditions. Particularly, the past twenty years have forced us to become aware of other customs, notions of family life different from our own, and the etymology of words we hardly knew before.

This chapter focuses on euphemisms that are meant to tone down oppressive and discriminatory acts toward women. Well-known euphemisms in connection with violence against women are *domestic dispute/ disturbance, domestic violence, family violence, violence in the family, violence-ridden families,* and *family conflicts,* all of which cover up who is the perpetrator and who is the victim. Some of them even cover up that it is about violence. The lack of a precise definition of a concept—especially concerning women and children in need—entails the risk that women will not receive the right aid and support. Ignorance may play an important role in how matters are handled. I will show that words matter in deciding what should be done, and what should not be done. More specifically, the use of euphemisms can obscure the cultural meaning of a concept, which may cause grim consequences for victims. In this sense, euphemisms can turn into dangerous words.

By definition, euphemisms do not disclose the meaning of a concept. Using euphemisms for foreign concepts may create even bigger problems when these are translated into a new cultural setting. Some concepts are completely new to the Danish cultural context—for example, *honor killing*: murdering women for male honor when women (allegedly) transgress gender borders. Other terms may be somewhat familiar, but often as obsolete memories of old times, as for instance *arranged marriage*.

In this chapter, I will focus on the terms *arranged marriage* and *honor killing* as two euphemisms for forms of violence against and suppression of women. The evidence I draw on includes scholarly literature, media reports, observations I made while working as a volunteer at the crisis center Danner House (a domestic violence shelter in Copenhagen), and interviews I conducted with women I met through Danner House and through my work as a consultant to an immigration attorney. All names of interviewees are pseudonyms.

From 1992 to 2007, my professional work involved applying for residence permits for many battered women, along with working on their divorce and custody cases. For six years (1992–98) I also worked at Danner House as a contact person[1] for foreign women and was active in political work on women's issues. Many of the women I met became very close to me. They allowed me to interview them and were happy to have a chance to tell their stories in detail. Some of the women I interviewed about their childhood, some about their lives in the village, some about why they refused to go to a shelter for foreign women only (as some leftist women advocated), about their married life in the extended family either here or in their homeland, virginity, how divorce procedures came about in their homeland (some had been married and divorced in their homeland, before they came to Denmark with a second husband), being forced to wear the veil, being a divorcee in an extended family, and how they are treated and so forth. What seemed most significant to me in these interviews was something that the Muslim women did not mention at all—namely, blaming themselves for having been battered (as Western women often do). Instead, the Muslim women seemed to have a quite different view of violent men that differed from the attitude of being an accessory to the crime (Mogensen 2007). Altogether, I worked with about 200 women, many of whom I interviewed (even though not always about the same theme).

The Danish Context

The debates in Denmark on whether a marriage was arranged or forced only very slowly came about at the beginning of the 1990s. The staff at crisis centers, who received the frightened girls that had escaped from home and often had been exposed to violence, were rather early in being aware that "arranged marriage" meant arranged by the parents and forced on a daughter.

However, social workers and the authorities named an unwanted marriage "arranged." *Forced marriage* was not a term used outside the crisis centers. In fact, if it was given a second thought at all, it was in terms of being so rare that it was hardly worth mentioning. There was, as such, a lot of confusion. What did it mean that a marriage was arranged, and when was a marriage forced? Was it at all possible to distinguish between the two?

The scholarly literature at the time did not do much to clear up the confusion. The same debates went on all over Scandinavia (see for instance Bredal 1998; Akpinar 1998; Kayed 1999). *Arranged marriage* was the common term for the marriages Muslim youth entered into. In a study by Norwegian researcher Anja Bredal (1998), young Muslims mentioned forced marriage only in passing. They considered the practice reprehensible but referred to it as other people's forced marriage, not their own. They were confident that when they were going to marry they would have a say, and that they would not accept force. Similarly, informants who were married already did not see themselves as victims of force. They seemed to distinguish between arranged and forced marriage based on whether they had openly opposed their parents' proposal or had given "a passive consent"— that is, not opposed their parents' proposal (Bredal 1998: 43). In the latter case, the youth defined the marriage as arranged.

Bredal's study also showed that while some minority youth rejected the idea of having parents choose their child's future spouse, others, especially young men, did not mind. If they did not have someone special in mind, they seemed not to care who they would marry. A reason could be that some young men have girlfriends their family will not allow them to marry. Therefore, they abide by their family's wishes but go on leading their lives as if they were not married, and place the newlywed (and immigrated) wife with her in-laws. Bredal seems to see a kind of "gray zone" in situations where young people do not want to marry but nevertheless—voluntarily or by force—abide by their parents' decision. After citing cases of women who had been forced to marry the man of their father's choice, Camilla Kayed (1999) concluded, "Most of my informants have thus entered an arranged marriage with more or less use of force."[2] In my opinion, *arranged* and *forced* are two mutually exclusive terms. Using them interchangeably only adds to the confusion.

Throughout the 1990s, as the number of adolescent girls and women escaping the threat of forced marriage increased, the topic of forced marriage and its consequences moved higher on the agenda. Successive governments passed several laws aimed at preventing forced marriage. In 2000, a section was added to the Penal Code stating that whoever forces a person to enter into marriage would face up to two years in prison. However, these legislative efforts to stop forced marriage did not really succeed.

In order to be able to legislate on forced marriage from an informed position, the government commissioned a survey from Socialforskningsinstituttet (Danish Institute of Social Research).[3] According to the survey, forced marriages were almost nonexistent in Denmark. In fact, the two researchers concluded that no more than 4 percent of the Danish Muslim minority women claimed to be forcibly married. In total, 628 participants had responded to questionnaires, and 88 qualitative interviews had been undertaken. The researchers argued that the small number of youth forced into marriage did not call for any legislation. However, it is important to know that most interviews took place with the whole family present, and that at the time the study was conducted, debates in the media on legislation to stop forced marriage were at their heights. That may have had an impact on the answers. The final report caused a public stir and was harshly criticized in the media.[4]

In 2009, Tina Magaard, on behalf of the Department of Equality under the Ministry of Welfare, conducted another survey. For the first time, Muslim women spoke for themselves about gender, culture, religion, and equality. Magaard's report showed that although the problem had been on the agenda and debated in public for a decade, the young women made it clear that the authorities still dealt with the matter of minority women escaping from forced marriage in the same way they had always done. Officials were still without much knowledge or consideration of the cultural problems the young women were facing when they refused to marry a man of their family's choice: "Not even psychologists have been educated to tackle these problems. They have come up with solutions like 'you can just do it anyway,' just as if I was an entirely Danish girl. I have been to five different psychologists, and none was educated within this area . . . There has been no help from the authorities . . . And the police are clear: 'You have to report him.' There has been no help" (an informant; 131; my translation).

This quotation shows that although the authorities may want to help, they very often do not have a clue as to the cultural norms the girls and women have to live by, and that they cannot just "do it anyway" or report a family member to the police.

Nongovernmental organizations also took part in the debates. IndSam[5] was the first Danish NGO to deal with this particular problem. An ad hoc group was set up at the end of the 1990s. The majority of the group, consisting mostly of officials from the Ministry of the Interior, the Migration Service, and high-ranking police officers, was reluctant to apply the notion of forced marriage. They preferred a "gray zone" approach, in which, if there was no proof of force, the marriage was considered arranged. Examples of what would have been considered proof of force included a woman reporting her parents to the police (a most unlikely occurrence) and a woman requesting that the Migration Service not grant a residence permit to the man she had been forcibly wed to during holidays in her parents' homeland. However, filing such a request would be a risky course of action, because a letter of refusal of residence permit is very detailed and a copy is sent to the woman making the request. Her parents would be likely to read the letter and learn of their daughter's action. What did not count as proof of force, though, was the fact that scared and abused girls and women ran away from home. This was considered a generational conflict. The young women would have to do what was most difficult for them: to provide "judicial proof," they would have to involve the Danish police and Migration Service.

The aim of IndSam was threefold: to protect girls and young women; to reach out to Muslim families in order to change their attitudes toward choosing whom their children would marry; and to amend the criminal law so that it would be a felony to force a young person into marriage.

In 2000, another Danish NGO, Broen (The Bridge), was established as a counseling center advising and aiding young minority women who were threatened to marry a man of their family's choice. Broen specifically put the freedom of choosing one's own marriage partner on the agenda. As Broen's members themselves were or had been victims of forced marriage, they did not use the terms *arranged marriage* or *gray zone*. To them, these terms were wrong because they only covered up the real problem.

For the first time, the grim consequences for girls opposing family decisions came to the fore. Having the attention of the politicians, Broen lobbied for stricter legislation and a special refuge for the young women, because the existing crisis centers and social centers did not know enough about the cultural and social implications of intervening in cases of forced marriage. In addition, because many young women were minors, the social system had to become involved.[6]

In legal terms there is no doubt whether a marriage is arranged or forced. Kirsten Ketscher, a professor at the Law Department (Retsvidenskabeligt Institut) at the University of Copenhagen,[7] explains the dichotomy between arranged and forced marriage: "In a judicial sense a marriage is only valid, if it is entered into freely by both parties. A marriage that has not been entered absolutely freely is forced marriage. There is nothing in between." Ketscher further refers to theUN Convention on the Elimination of All Forms of Discrimination against Women (which Denmark has adopted), which states that a valid marriage requires both parties' "free and unconditional consent." Distinguishing between arranged and forced marriages cannot be under discussion. Ketscher argues that Garbi Schmidt and Vibeke Jakobsen favor abusers over victims when they say that the youth they had interviewed had entered into marriage out of love and that therefore no further legislation was necessary.

The Problem of What Constitutes Appropriate Support

Many girls, before they ran away from home and sought refuge at a crisis center, asked for help from social services. However, because they were unable to convince the social workers of the significant cultural implications of an arranged marriage, social workers would advise the girls to firmly say no to their parents' proposal. The social workers did not understand the fuss these girls were making. Instead, they thought the girls were overly dramatic when they said that refusal to abide by family rules might cause gross violence. It has taken years for the authorities (and social workers and teachers) to understand at least some of the consequences for adolescents who oppose family decisions. Instead, the problems have been seen in terms of passing conflicts between generations that eventually would "go away." If the girls or women insisted they could not go home, the authorities would help them to a safe place such as a crisis center and then inform the parents that their daughter was safe and in the care of the authorities.

As cited before, "there has been no help from the authorities." The dilemma is that the girls and women want the authorities to intervene, but by engaging the authorities they breach the first rule in the book, which is not to spread family secrets, and especially not to the authorities. Doing so may escalate the conflicts between family members and the young. Fatiha, a participant in Bredal's study, suggests that a "place to talk" might help, where mediation between the parents and the daughter may take place at a very early stage of the conflict. However, mediation places would have to be set up by the authorities. Fatiha is aware of the risk such involvement of outsiders may entail, and that the parents may send their daughter abroad in order to undermine the "helpers" (Bredal 1998: 87f.).

The debate on whether a marriage is arranged or forced will probably go on for years to come. Meanwhile, however, safe havens for young women and for young couples who escape forced marriage have been provided along with legislation that might help Muslim youth.

Migrant Women on Forced Marriage

Even while the extent of force against female descendants of immigrants was acknowledged, the plight of immigrant wives was ignored. Forced marriage was considered a "domestic" phenomenon—that is, one pertaining only to young women brought up in Denmark, not to foreign women. The latter were believed to have accepted their marriage freely and left their countries, families, and friends willingly to settle down in a foreign country with a husband they did not know. The strongest voice in these debates was probably the Norwegian author and journalist Hege Storhaug, who worked for the organization Human Rights Service Norway and had lived in Pakistan for three years (1996–98). In several studies, published in 1998, 2003, and 2006, Storhaug showed that, contrary to the assumption by politicians that third-generation immigrants no longer get married to young people from their grandparents' village, these transnational marriages were in fact increasing with each generation. Transnational marriages seemed to be systematized in the sense of systematically and deliberately matching a boy or girl from a village in the country of origin with a youth in Denmark (see also Akpinar 1998: 58).

Upon arrival as a bride in a new country, many female marriage-migrants face the problem that their husband was not interested in getting married at all, and certainly not to a woman from his parents' or grandparents' village. He very often has a girlfriend whom he is not allowed to marry. Aylin Akpinar (1998) relates the story of Turkish-Kurdish Semra. Semra talks about her husband who had a Swedish girlfriend when his family forced him to marry her. Semra did not like him but gave in. She was 15 years old and was with her in-laws first in Turkey and later in Sweden. She pleaded with her father not to be forced to go to Sweden, but to no avail (58).

Pakistani Fatima, who was also placed with her in-laws when she arrived in Denmark, told me after her divorce, "I was married, my husband was not."[8] Her husband had a Danish girlfriend and did not want to marry Fatima. She hardly ever saw him. When she did he would beat her up. When they are divorced, most migrant women say that their husband also had been forcibly married, but they also believe that he could have refused with impunity. In doing so, the young men would save the women from all the despair they suffer if the marriage does not work out. However, for a young man to refuse his parents' proposal with impunity is not always possible. In recent years, it has come to the authorities' attention that young men also risk being threatened if they disobey their families' wishes. One of Bredal's interviewees, Khalid, said that he did not know he was going to marry until his father told him that the family had found a wife for him and that he was engaged to her and going to live in Norway. Khalid accepted a decision that was already made: "We are used to it, do not think about it, it is the parents' duty" (Bredal 1998, 45f.). He went on to say that he did not know what would happen if he had refused, but he would anticipate great problems. However, because he accepted, he did not think he had been forced.

From my interviews with women, it appears that with the exception of a few well-educated women from capital cities and wealthy families, all had been forced to marry the strange man their families had chosen for them. The force involved may not have been physical violence, but psychological pressure can be as hard or harder. The idea of being responsible for the common good of the whole family applies even more to women than to men. It is almost impossible to go against the pressure of knowing that her whole family will fall apart should she refuse their wishes.

If a marriage-migrant left a violent husband while still without a residence permit in her own right, she would be expelled from the country (Mogensen 1994). According to crisis centers and women's organizations, this was de facto punishment of women for being battered and constituted a legalization of the violence. To improve the legal rights of female marriage-migrants, the organizations demonstrated against the expulsion of battered women. They also collected signatures from the public. The politicians were seen as the violent men's extended arm. The debates in the media went high, and nonprofessionals as well as experts on law and migration participated in the debates. At the end of 1993, the Ministry of Interior set up a committee (Kvindeudvalget; The Woman Committee) to strengthen battered immigrant women's legal rights. On July 1, 1996, a protection clause in the Alien Act for these women came into power.[9]

After the law had come into power, more battered women came to the crisis centers in the hope that they would obtain a residence permit on the grounds of violence. In the application for the permit, the women had to disclose every detail about their family circumstances in their homeland. Despite the political fight for foreign women's protection against expulsion, forced marriage was not on the agenda at all. Most significant to me was that, with few exceptions, the women did not know the man they married. To me, it was obvious that these women were in the same situation as the young women of minority descent who tried to escape forced marriage, and I became interested in the circumstances pertaining to the marriages of marriage migrants. Many of them agreed to be interviewed by me on how their marriage came about.

These interviews showed me that most migrant women distinguished between arranged and forced marriage the same way as Danish Muslim women. To them, too, it was a matter of whether or not they submitted to their parents' wishes. When they had agreed with their parents' proposal, or when their consent had been "silent," they would not see themselves as victims of forced marriage, even though they opposed the marriage. Three women, Fatima from Pakistan, Ayse from Turkey, and Nilüfar from Iran, denied having been forced.

> *Fatima*: I said yes to my father, but I cried and cried and cried to my mother.
> Q: Why did you cry?
> F: I did not want to marry him. I did not want to leave my country and my family.
> Q: Why did you accept then?
> F: I was afraid to say no. I was afraid my father might hit me.
> Q: Has your father ever hit you?
> F: No, never. He is a very good man. He has never hurt anyone of us, but all of us have always complied with his wishes. Therefore, I did not know what would happen, if I opposed him.

Ayse: I loathed him from first sight. My older sister and I were sitting on the couch waiting for him to choose which one of us he wanted for a wife. He wanted us to stand up, and he chose me, because I was the tallest.

Q: Why did you accept?

A: My mother, a widow with five underaged children, told me that I was free to refuse him, but that it was very difficult for her to go on maintaining us all on her small pension. I had to relieve some of the burden on my mother.

Nilüfar: I did not like him at all.

Q: Then why did you accept to marry him?

N: His mother called my mother (both widows) on the phone and wanted me for her son. I had seen him a few times at family gatherings and never liked him. My mother handed me the phone and told me to choose for myself. His mother put a lot a pressure on me. As they lived many hours by bus from our home, she said that she wanted my answer on the phone. They did not intend to make such a long journey if I refused. I was 18 years old and it was the first time in my life I had to make a decision on my own. I could not refuse her. I am brought up to respect older people. I had to comply. It was not my mother forcing me. You can say I had only myself to blame.

These cases are seemingly close to Bredal's "gray zone" approach. "The common good of the family" is a very strong factor to make the women comply. Fear, whether imaginary or real, of what might happen if they refuse to comply may also play a role. However, refusal is rarely an option to youth living in small villages or rural places in Muslim countries.

While these women did not blame their acceptance of an unwanted marriage on their parents, Suzan from Iran, who was under the same psychological pressure to marry, did recognize this pressure as force, even though she agreed:

When I had poured tea[10] for him and his parents, I went back into the kitchen. My mother came and said that they had accepted me for their son. I burst into tears. He was fat and ugly, not at all a man I would like to marry. At first, my mother laughed and said that it does not matter how a person looks. When I went on crying, she told me that a refusal would cause my father a heart attack and then we would all live in the street. My father had been married before and the son of his first marriage would inherit our house. How could I refuse then? First, I would cause my father's death and then my mother, younger siblings and I would live in the street. I had to comply in order to save my family. However, I was surely forced into that marriage.

Bredal (1998) also mentions the mother's use of the "father will be sick" phrase as a part of the psychological pressure to make the young comply (47).

Generally, if parents put pressure on a woman to marry and the marriage fails, they often support her wish to divorce. However, it is usually on the condition that she does not come back to her homeland. Having a divorced woman in the home is considered so shameful that her family will usually accept her choice of a second husband almost regardless of who he is. Although family, friends, and others know that a daughter in one particular family has been divorced, it seems that if she remarries and—even better—is out of sight, she is also out of mind, and the shame "goes away." In Bredal's study, Muhammed explains that after his sister's divorce, his parents were happy to accept her own choice for her second husband (47).

In a personal conversation I had with Sahar from Syria, she told me that she had been forcibly married to a man in her homeland and then divorced. She herself chose her second husband, a Syrian living in Denmark, and her older brother immediately accepted her choice. Her family had been rather reluctant to take her in after her divorce, so when she divorced her second, very violent husband in Denmark, and had still not obtained a residence permit in her own right, she was in despair.

> Q: Do you want to go back or do you want to try to apply for residence permit on the grounds of cruelty?
> Sahar: I have to stay. I cannot go back. After my first divorce, my family took me in, because they had forced me to marry. This time the choice was mine and they will not feel responsible. I know they will not let me in.

In the West, young Muslims may be allowed to choose their own future spouse, but Leila, one of Bredal's informants, points out that the parents' consent to the marriage is vital. Without it, parents will not take responsibility if the marriage fails (1998: 55). Several of the youth in Bredal's research expressed this sentiment. They believe that if the parents' choice proves to be wrong, the parents would be an accessory to the failed marriage (25).

In the women's homeland, force used against them seems to be mostly of a psychological character. However, in the West, force against a women (and sometimes against a man, too) who refuses or is reluctant to marry seems to be more physical and often involves extreme violence, death threats, confinement, and ostracism (Storhaug 1998; 2006; Eldén 2001;

Larsen 2004; Danneskiold-Samsøe et al. 2011). A reason for these different reactions from the families may be that in the homeland the young person has nowhere to turn for support: neither family members nor the authorities. Therefore psychological pressure to do the right thing for the good of the family will usually make young people comply. In contrast, it seems as if young women brought up in the West are less likely to succumb to the cultural thinking of "for the sake of the family." In addition, families may suspect, especially in recent years, that teachers and social workers may help the young people to a safe place, and that ultimately police and the legal system may also become involved. Under these conditions, families apparently resort to intimidation and often severe violence to stop the adolescents from involving the authorities, which would bring shame on the whole family.

The much harsher behavior toward adolescents brought up in the West seems above all due to promises their fathers made to the extended family or friends in the homeland that they will help their sons or daughters to the West when they have come of age. Although family means everything to the adolescents, it seems that many of them are nonetheless opposed to the idea that they could be held responsible for a promise their father gave to a person in the extended family in the parents' country of origin.

Over the past years, Danish Muslim youth have begun to marry with other Danish Muslims and in many cases postpone marriage until their mid-twenties.[11] The improved educational level among Muslim youth, especially women, may also play an important role in the shift toward marrying later and marrying a partner of one's choice. However, there are still many youngsters who are forcibly married to unknown men or women from their parents' country of origin.[12]

In recent years there seems to have been a shift from the dichotomy of arranged/forced marriage to the dichotomy of forced/love marriage. The shift may have been caused by several factors. In addition to those mentioned in the previous paragraph, legal changes may have played a role. Due to many amendments to the Alien Act, it is now rather difficult to meet the conditions under which one can have a spouse imported from the parents' homeland. Hence more young people find their spouse in Denmark. Some of these marriages may be love marriages. However, as the shelter RED in 2010 was expanded to receive couples fleeing forced marriage, there is evidence that some parents still refuse to accept that their daughters or sons fall in love and choose their own spouse (Danneskiold-Samsøe et al. 2011).

Discourses on "Honor Killing" versus the Liquidation of Women

The term *honor killing* was very little debated until after the millennium, although between 1986 and 2005 17 women (and one boy in 1985) in Denmark had been killed.[13] The authorities and people in general were, and many still are, unaware of the basic cultural and social implications, as well as the conspiracy within the family that precedes such killings. Hence the killings were referred to by the familiar yet ill-fitting term *homicide* with the consequence that only the person who actually committed the murder was convicted. The term, and especially the word *honor*, was often debated in the media, not least after the liquidation of Ghazala in 2005 (this will be detailed in a following section). The debaters failed to see the "honor" in these killings. In March 2006 the activist group Women for Freedom (Kvinder for Frihed) was established, and one of the group's first actions was to go through all euphemisms that are disguising the suppression of women and therefore harmful. For instance, the group advocated changing *honor killing* to *woman liquidation* in order to clarify who is being killed and that conspiracy is an important ingredient of the killing.[14]

The liquidations of women in Scandinavia[15] caused some soul searching on the part of the countries' authorities. Recognizing that these women need protection, the police in Denmark established a national strategy in 2007 for a preventive effort in cases where a felony had not yet been committed (Kliver 2008: 67).

The cases of the Fadime and Ghazala liquidations are discussed in detail in this chapter to demonstrate the elements that can lead to murder: the police's refusal to aid women who ask for help because their lives are threatened, the shame spread, nonobedience to an ostracizing order issued by the family,[16] the women's need for reconciliation with their family, and female members who trick the eloped women in order for the men to be able to get to them and kill them.

Two Kinds of Honor: Şeref *and* Namus

When using the euphemism of *honor killing*, one has to be aware of the confusion this creates when notions of honor are transplanted into a different cultural setting. In Bredal's opinion, "[t]raditional criteria cannot simply be transplanted into a new context." (1998: 34).

Leylâ Pervizat (2003), whose research on honor killing focuses on four districts in Turkey, offers some explanation as to why the term is problematic. Pervizat argues that there are two different kinds of honor in Islam: *şeref* (in Arabic sharaf) and *namus* (in Arabic ird). The former is a man's honor and exists only vis-à-vis other men. Once a man loses *şeref* the possibility for regaining it is next to nil. *Namus* depends on female shame/dishonor—that is, the (sexual) conduct of women—and is a matter for the whole family. Although *şeref* and *namus* are separate concepts, they are also intertwined, so that if a man is dishonored by a female member of his family, he will also lose his *şeref*.

Mükerem Wigur (personal conversation) explains how *şeref* and *namus* work in the provincial town in Anatolia, Turkey, where she grew up: *şeref* (honor) is something a man has but will lose if he acts in a dishonorable way. He will become *şerefsiz* (without honor) in the eyes of other men. *Namus* (shame/dishonor) is something that will hit a man through shameful behavior of female members of his family. He then becomes *namussuz* (shamed/dishonored). He can lose his *şeref* in two ways: by either lying, stealing, being untruthful, or so on toward his family or friends, in which case his *şeref* is lost forever—or if he is *namussuz*. In the latter case, he may regain his *şeref* by getting rid of his *namus*. This could be achieved by ostracizing or killing the woman who is seen to have dishonored the men in her family.

Although ostracism may be common in bigger towns or cities in Turkey, in provincial towns and villages, according to Wigur, it rarely is an option. Here the woman most likely is killed. Pervizat's research corroborates this statement. In Turkish, murdering a woman for male honor is called *namus cinayeti* (literally, shame killing). Honor killing in Turkish is *şeref cinayeti*, which means one man killing another man for honor. Pervizat defines the so-called honor killing as extrajudicial execution, and execution outside law is liquidation. There are some, though, who name the killing *execution*, but this is not the right term. *Execution* is a judicial term and thereby renders the term an air of legality.

More often than not, Pervizat puts *honor killing* in quotation marks or precedes *honor* with a "so-called." Many researchers,[17] journalists, politicians, and others have adopted the same usage, either in want of a more appropriate concept or for reluctance to call a spade a spade. *Killing* has negative connotations, but when combined with the positive term *honor*, the resulting expression is counteracted or neutralized (Bjarnason 2006: 88).

I see the application of quotation marks being a call to the reader to be aware of the incompatibility of the combined term.

Unni Wikan, too, defines *şeref* as a man's sense of honor and self-worth, and *namus* as the purity and propriety of women (2003: 67). Male honor is irretrievably linked to female (potential) shame. However, Wikan criticizes the tendency to use the phrase "so-called honor killing." She believes that it is a demonstration of disassociation of the act, as *honor* typically has positive connotations. She argues that one ought to use the term *honor killing* (plain and simple) to be able to "face the fact in order to be able to get rid of such atrocities" (20). I fail to see how an apparently misleading phrase should enable one to understand what she calls the "iron logic" of a certain term (166). I argue that such logic has escaped the comprehension of the authorities and the public. On the contrary, few seem to see any logic in connecting *honor* and *killing*. Counter to her argument, Wikan mentions Kurdo Baksi, a Swedish-Kurdish debater and author, who is opposing the term *honor killing* and advocating the term *shame killing* (20, note 1). Although favoring the term *honor killing*, Wikan herself uses different terms, such as *murder* and *liquidation* (see for instance 27).

As will become clear in the next section, the positive connotations that the word *honor* may lend to the term *honor killing* have had devastating consequences for women asking for protection. In concordance with Pervizat, I argue that such killing is extrajudicial. As such, there is no other term than *liquidation* to describe these killings. Further, *honor killing* is not the term for liquidation of a woman by her relatives but for one man killing another man for honor.

Confusion of Terms

Being unfamiliar with the cultural implications of *namus*, some Danish psychologists have proposed that the murder of a woman on leaving her partner (sometimes named *separation assault* in the Western literature— see Humphreys 1999; Ekbrand 2006) is equivalent to the killing that is meant to restore a man's and/or a family's honor. The psychologists argue that if a (non-Muslim) man kills his wife (and more often than not his children, too) and then commits suicide, he is overwhelmed with the same urge to restore his honor as his Muslim counterpart. There is a lot to be said against this idea. In the cases in which these murderers did not commit suicide, they talk about jealousy and how they snapped when the woman wanted a divorce. Evidently, rage, and not restoring honor, is the background for these murders. Further, the killing is decided and carried out by the man only.

Mehmet Ümit Necef, associate professor at the Centre for Middle Eastern Studies at Southern-Danish University, strongly rejects the parallel between *crime of passion* and *honor killing*. In a column in *Weekendavisen* no. 18 (April 30–May 1, 2008), he quotes the Turkish woman's human rights defender Jülide Aral, who explained the difference between the two notions. *Crime of passion* lacks several components of *honor killing*: an applauding audience, the killing being collectively decided and planned, the murderer being collectively chosen, and the acceptance and support of the killing from the women in the family.

These elements are not present in a (non-Muslim) murderer's case. If the potential murderer's surroundings become aware of his intentions, anything will be done to safeguard the woman (and children). According to media reports of cases in which a woman (and her children) had been killed, family and friends claimed that they tried to warn the woman, often for years. Similarly, in the crisis center we often had mothers who urged us to prevent the woman from going back to the man.

The liquidation of a woman who transgresses is a "family matter" caused by the feeling of having to live with *namussuz* because of a female member's noncompliance with the will of her family. As such, the killing "is not about rejected love or relationship. It is about the collective's rights and the individual's duty to submission" (Wikan 2003: 22).

No matter how abominable any kind of murder, one must keep in mind that what is lost in translation here, both linguistically and culturally, is the key notion of conspiracy. Killing a woman for transgressing gender borders needs an approving audience who share the same view. The woman's (alleged) conduct that caused the loss of her family's *şeref* may trigger the idea of killing her, but the conspiracy is the necessary means to carry out the liquidation (see also Souad 2003: 118).

Control through Slander

Fear plays a vital role, in that when a female in the family violates the norms, the entire family will fear being exposed to slander and ostracized by the whole community. A common strategy to keep women within the borders of proper gender norms appears to be control through slander. In her research on migrant Pakistanis in Britain and France, Pnina Werbner (2007: 166) explains the necessity for women of being modestly dressed in order not to fall prey to slander. Gossip is dangerous, not only for a woman, but also for her family, whose reputation is at risk. They are "words . . . that seem to come from nowhere," as Jacqueline Rose (2009: 2–3) puts it. Slander can also cause other people's exclusion of the family: "Such exclusion is a form of social death." Social death is a condition a family will go far to avoid, even to the brink of murder and beyond.

Rose argues that the starting point and preconditions for the killings are rumors and gossip. She illustrates this with the case of Heshu, who repeatedly informed her teachers about her fear of being forcibly married. Not only did they ignore her, but they informed her parents about her (Christian Lebanese) boyfriend. Her father eventually killed her (2009: 1). Suspicion of having done something wrong is enough to get killed (Storhaug 1998: 31). An informant in Magaard's report put it this way: "It is the slander that can cause a girl to lose her life. Because of ignorance and the parents' priorities, a murder can happen" (2009: 127). Another informant said to Magaard: "I actually feared death" (132).[18]

Ostracism

If a woman refuses to marry the man of the family's choice, this proves to others that the family has no control over her. If the daughter cannot be called to order, a marriage promise given to a family member or friend in the parents' homeland may need to be broken. The woman's nonacceptance of being forcibly married then becomes a precondition for liquidation. However, a family, depending on its socioeconomic and educational level, may choose ostracism over liquidation. Ostracism literally means to be excluded—expelled from the home/community—but in Western countries, it seems not uncommon for a young Muslim woman to ostracize herself, so to speak, by running away from home. If the woman suspects that she will be "dumped" during holiday in her parents' homeland, then "self-ostracism" may be a way to avoid this (Danneskiold-Samsøe et al. 2011: 14).

What measures could be considered in these cases? Ostracism and liquidation against a transgressing woman depend on several factors. One concerns the issue of who is aware that the family has lost control of the woman. Is the family secret still kept within the family, has it already spread to the neighborhood, or has it even reached the attention of the extended family abroad? According to Wikan (2003: 11), shame does not affect honor until it has become public. It is not necessary to take action until the family secret has become public knowledge.

In the West, if the family decides to take action against a woman, it most likely will opt for ostracism. Several conditions are attached to the decision. The ostracized woman must keep out of the sight and life of her family and friends forever (Wikan 2003: 167). Family members are warned not to get in touch with her or respond to her should she try to make contact. She may be killed if the family secret is revealed to outsiders, or if she is not abiding by the family's decision of ostracism. In this way, ostracism may precede liquidation should the ostracized woman breach the rules.

Spreading the Secret

Some of the young women explained that when asking for any kind of help, the social workers would offer to talk to the family (Magaard 2009). The social workers do not understand why their offer is vigorously refused by the girls or women, who are forbidden in particular to disclose family secrets to the Danish authorities. Offers to talk to the family terrify the women (Wincentz Andersen 2008: 99). The young women know the combination of transgression and disclosing this family secret may tip the balance from ostracism to liquidation (Wikan 2003; Eldén 2001).

Case accounts of liquidated women show what can happen when women try to contact their family through female family members, including the mother, after they had been ostracized or had escaped from home. In these cases, this step proved to be fatal, as will be seen in both the Fadime and Ghazala cases. Media accounts of the two cases show that female members of the family sided with the men's decision and lured the ostracized women into a trap so that the family member chosen to liquidate them could get close to them. The fact that the women, even under the threat of death, could not stay away from their family demonstrates how painful it is to lose one's entire family, along with one's cultural roots. The deeply felt need to be reconciled with their family urges these women to make contact even though their lives are in jeopardy (Khader 2000: 182; Wincentz Andersen 2008: 101). The loss of family can also be devastating to young men, who want reconciliation with their family as much as the women (Storhaug 1998: 38).

Ignorance of these cultural implications has imperiled women's lives and is the reason women whose lives are threatened are thought to be excessively dramatic and hence not credible. It took horrible crimes to convince the authorities that these women were not overstating their case but that their lives really were in imminent danger. The Fadime liquidation in Sweden in 2002 was followed closely in the Danish media, but for one reason or another, the killing sank into oblivion until the liquidation of Ghazala in Denmark in 2005.

The Liquidations of Fadime and Ghazala

Although the background of the parents of Swedish-Kurdish Fadime and Danish-Pakistani Ghazala was rather similar—they respectively came from small villages in the Kurdish part of Turkey and the Punjab province of Pakistan—the young women's countries of upbringing were quite different. Fadime was brought up and had her schooling and education in Sweden. She was a modern young woman and refused to live by the traditional rules of her parents' Kurdish village, which expected her to marry a cousin of her parents' choice. Ghazala, on the other hand, was brought up in a Pakistani village and came to Denmark only once a year on visits. She knew of no other life than the traditions in the village.[19]

Fadime

The modern life that Fadime wanted to lead was miles away from the traditional life of her family. When her father discovered that she had a relationship with Swedish-Iranian Patrick, she received death threats from both her father and brother (the real names of the individuals involved in the case have been in the media and several books have been written about the court cases of both killings). She knew her life was in danger, but when she turned to the police for help, she was refused. Fadime herself went to the media, including television, to the police, and to Parliament to try to stop the violence Muslim women in general were exposed to: "I was alarmed that the police did not take me seriously. To them my story was like a fabricated fairytale. Their only advice to me was that I should go home to my family and tell them that it was illegal to threaten me and that they should respect the Swedish law and traditions. The police did not understand the seriousness of my situation, and their folly led from my point of view to a disrespectful and insulting behavior" (My translation; Wincentz Andersen 2008: 99).

Fadime's brother physically attacked her in the street in 1998, and she was severely injured and hospitalized. Her brother was sentenced to 5 months in prison.

Fadime and Patrick[20] moved to another town. Her father told her not to come back to Uppsala. If she did not obey, she would be killed. In Fadime's mind, the safest way to avoid being killed was to tell about her life in the media. She was on television several times. In addition, she talked to about 350 people in Parliament in November 2001 (Wikan 2003: 229). She also wanted to give voice to other girls who lived under duress. Far from saving her life, it seems that this public disclosure of "family secrets" and "soiling" of the family name further enraged her family members. During the last year of her life, after having reconciled with her mother, she met a few times with her mother and two of her sisters in the apartment of one of the sisters.

Someone gave Fadime away. It was probably no accident that her father and brother knew about these visits with her mother and two sisters, although they were rare (only a few times during one year) and very irregular. From the police interrogation record of Fadime's 13-year-old sister Nabile (reported in Wikan 2003, chapter 8), it seems most likely that it was Nabile who informed her brother of Fadime's whereabouts. Nabile told the police that she had asked him if he would hurt Fadime, and that he denied having any such thing on his mind. Nabile did not believe her brother would harm Fadime. She did not believe he ever did, and she believed that Fadime was lying when she filed a complaint with the police.

In her father and brother's opinion, Fadime violated all the rules in the book. She refused to marry her cousin in Turkey and wanted to choose her own husband. She filed a complaint with the police against her brother and he went to prison. She spread the family secrets so effectively that all television viewers in the country came to know the name of the family. She violated the family's order of ostracism. She did so in opposition to rules that she, as a young, modern, Swedish woman, did not want to live by.

Ghazala

Ghazala's upbringing in a small traditional village in Pakistan was far from the life of a woman in a modern city in the West. She did not speak Danish and she knew little, if anything at all, about Denmark. She was only in Denmark once a year and knew nobody apart from her closest family. It was on her annual flight in 2001 from Islamabad to Copenhagen that she met Danish-Afghan Emal. They fell in love. She told her mother she had met an Afghan man in whom she was interested. She was beaten up and was told there was no way the family would accept him as her husband. In her family cousin-marriages were the norm. However, the young people kept in touch by cellphone and emails. When Ghazala visited Denmark again on September 4, 2005, they decided to elope (Wincentz Andersen 2008: 80). In the early morning on September 5, 2005, she left her brother's house.

While the young people were on the run, the family started searching for her. In the absence of the father, the brother had full responsibility for Ghazala. That is maybe why he took the rather unusual and desperate measure of "spreading the secret" outside of the family. The father was a taxi-company owner, and all the men in the family worked as taxi drivers, and other Pakistani men were employed there as well. They were all summoned in order to look out for Ghazala. After a few days without any trace of her, the brother had to inform his father of the incident, and the father immediately came to Denmark.

Ghazala confided in her aunt (her father's sister) in the hope that her aunt could influence her father, so that the couple would be forgiven. Instead, her aunt kept the family informed of the steps the couple took to hide. On September 11, the father turned up at one of the homes where the young couple had been hiding for a few nights, and he learned they had been there, but had moved on. In a subsequent family meeting, it was decided that the brother was to do the actual killing and family members and employees would chase the couple. The aunt who was already in connection with Ghazala should keep the family informed of their whereabouts and lure the couple into to a place where they could be killed. Ghazala, who hoped for reconciliation with her family, was easily lured.

On September 23, 2005, her brother liquidated Ghazala in the street. Her husband (the couple had been married for only two days) survived but was severely injured. When questioned by police at the hospital after his surgery, Emal told the police that they had been asking for help at four police stations around the country, but in vain. No one took their story seriously.

For the first time it was disclosed in court how such a conspiracy works, and how the whole family, and in this case also the family's friends and father's employees, conspired to kill a young woman who had married a man of her own choice. As the whole story of the liquidation of Ghazala was recounted in court, it was clear that it involved a cold-blooded conspiracy to kill the woman and her husband. If a woman's entire family is conspiring to liquidate her, and if she cannot obtain any aid and support from society, she has very little chance to escape the fate her family has plotted for her.[21]

Conclusion

It has taken almost two decades to appreciate that forced marriage and arranged marriage are two very different marriages. Not to comply with a forced marriage may precede liquidation. Arranged marriage is a marriage where families make all the arrangements after a woman and man freely and with their full consent have chosen to marry each other. Slowly, traditions change and some couples can choose and marry each other with their parents' consent. However, there are still couples who run away and hide for fear of the consequences of transgressing the traditions of their families. There are also still youngsters who are forced to marry an unknown man/woman from their parents' homeland, even though this problem has diminished to some extent through laws. The two cases recounted show that police and the authorities in general failed to protect the two women out of ignorance of the cultural dynamics underlying these liquidations. Tragic incidents (running away, going into hiding, being ostracized, being killed) have occurred exactly because the phenomena were not named appropriately.

In concordance with Bredal, I argue that it is difficult to transplant foreign cultural norms into a new context. When three individuals—Leylâ Pervizat, Mükerem Wigur, and Kurdo Baksi (in Wikan), all brought up in countries with a tradition of liquidating gender transgressing women—dismiss that *honor killing* has anything to do with men killing women, and when writers, researchers, and reporters apparently are in want of a more adequate translation, it may be time to abolish the term *honor killing* altogether. The term *liquidation* will make the authorities understand the imminent danger threatened women face and thus will benefit them.

References

Akpinar, Aylin. (1998). *Male's Honor and Female's Shame. Gender and Ethnic identity Constructions among Turkish Divorcees in the Migration Context.* PhD Dissertation, Department of Sociology, Uppsala University.

Ali, Ayaan Hirsi. (2005). *Jeg anklager (I accuse).* Copenhagen: Jyllands-Postens Forlag.

Banks, Emily, Olav Meirik, Tim Farley, Oluwole Akande, Heli Bathija, and Mohamed Ali. (2006). "Female Genital Mutilation and Obstetric Outcome: WHO Collaborative Prospective Study in Six African Countries." *The Lancet* 367 (9525): 1835–41.

Bjarnason, Nina. (2006). "Sådan kan du bekæmpe eufemismer—analyser og angreb" ("How to Fight Euphemisms—Analyses and Attacks"). In Vibeke Manniche (ed.), *Maskeret tvang—en antologi (Masked Force—An Antology)*, 84–95. Holte: Forlaget LIVA.

Bredal, Anja. (1998). "Arrangerte ekteskap og tvangsekteskap blant ungdom med innvandrer-bakgrunn" ("Arranged Marriages and Forced Marriages among Youth with Immigration Background"). Extended essay, Kompetansesenter for likestilling, Oslo.

Danneskiold-Samsøe, Sofie, Yvonne Mørck, and Bo Wagner Sørensen. (2011). *"Familien betyder alt": Vold mod kvinder i etniske minoritetsfamilier (The Family Means Everything: Violence against Women in Ethnic Minority Families)*. Frederiksberg: Frydenlund.

Ekbrand, Hans. (2006). *Separationer och mäns våld mot kvinnor (Separations and Men's Violence against Women)*. PhD Dissertation, Sociologiska Institutionen, Göteborg Universitet.

Eldén, Åsa. (2001). "En berättelse om tvång och frihet: Kontext, mening, identitetsskapande" ("A Narrative on Force and Freedom: Context, Meaning, Identity Creation"). *Kvinneforskning* 25 (2): 50–62.

Eldén, Åsa, and Jenny Westerstrand, eds. (2007). *Guts and Glory: Festskrift till Eva Lundgren*. Uppsala: Uppsala Universitet.

Güvercile, Sengül. (2003). *Æresdrab (Honor Killing)*. Oslo: Aschehoug.

Humphreys, Catherine. (1999). "Judicial Alienation Syndrome—Failures to Respond to Post-separation Violence." *Family Law Journal* 29: 313–16.

Kayed, Camilla. (1999). "Rett, religion og byråkrati: En studie av skilsmisse blant muslimer I Norge" ("Law, Religion and Bureaucracy: A Study of Divorce among Muslims in Norway"). Extended essay, Institutt og museum for antropologi, Universitetet i Norge.

Khader, Naser, with Jakob Kvist. (2000). *khader.dk*. Copenhagen: Aschehoug Dansk Forlag.

158   BRITTA MOGENSEN

Kjær, Pia. (2006). *Elskerinde i Allahs verden* (*Mistress in Allah's World*). Århus: Forlaget SIESTA.

Kliver, Dorte. (2008). "Konfliktmægling—set ud fra et politimæssigt synspunkt" ("Conflict mediation—from the police force's point of view"). In Arne Schmidt Møller (ed.), *Når æren er på spil—guidelines mod æresforbrydelser* (*When Honor Is at Stake—Guidelines against Honor Crimes*), 67–78. Århus: SIESTA.

Magaard, Tina. (2009). "At være muslimsk kvinde i Danmark" ("Being a Muslim Woman in Denmark"). The Department of Equality under the Ministry of Welfare.

Mogensen, Britta. (1994). "Voldsramt og udvisningstruet—et dobbelt overgreb" ("Battered and under Threat of Expulsion—A Double Assault"). *Jordens Folk* 29 (3): 102–5.

Mogensen, Britta. (2007). "Vold i et flerkulturelt perspektiv—mellemøstlige kvinder fortæller" ("Violence in a Multicultural Perspective—Middle Eastern Women Speak"). In Åsa Eldén and Jenny Westerstrand (eds.), *Guts and Glory: Festskrift till Eva Lundgren*, 35–54. Uppsala: Uppsala Universitet.

Nøhr Larsen, Marianne. (2004). *De små oprør—tanker og metoder i arbejdet med minoritetspiger* (*Small Revolts—Thoughts and Methods on the Work with Minority Girls*). Århus: Aarhus Universitetsforlag.

Osmani, Nadije. (2000). *Forbandede ære* (*Damned Honor*). Århus: CDR-Forlag.

Pervizat, Leylâ. (2003). "In the Name of Honor." *Human Rights Dialogue* 2 (10): 30–31.

Rashid, Rushy. (2000). *Et løft af sløret* (*Lifting the Veil*). Copenhagen: Gyldendal.

Rose, Jaqueline. (2009). "A Piece of White Silk." *London Review of Books* 31 (21): 5–8.

Schmidt, Garbi, and Vibeke Jakobsen. (2004). *Pardannelse blandt etniske minoriter i Danmark* (*Couple Relationships among Ethnic Minorities in Denmark*). Copenhagen: Socialforskningsinstituttet.

Schmidt Møller, Arne. (2006). *Ghazala—et æresdrab i Danmark* (*Ghazala— An Honor Killing in Denmark*). Århus: Forlaget SIESTA.

Souad. (2003). *Levende Brændt* (*Burned Alive*). Copenhagen: Møntergården.

Storhaug, Hege. (1998). *Hellig tvang: Unge norske muslimer om kjærlighet og ekteskap* (*Holy Force: Young Norwegian Muslims on Love and Marriage*). Oslo: Kagge Forlag.

Storhaug, Hege. (2003). *Feminin integrering—utfordringer i et fleretnisk samfunn* (*Feminine Integration—Challenges in a Multiethnic Society*). Norge: KOLOFON A/S.

Storhaug, Hege. (2006). *Men Størst Av Alt Er Friheten: Om innvandringens konsekvenser* (*The Greatest of All Is Freedom: On the Consequences of Immigration*). Oslo: Kagge Forlag.

Werbner, Pnina. (2007). "Veiled Intervention in Pure Space: Honor, Shame and Embodied Struggles among Muslims in Britain and France." *Theory, Culture & Society* 24 (2): 161–86.

Wikan, Unni. (2003). *Ære og drab: Fadime—en sag til eftertanke* (*Honor and Murder: Fadime—A Case for Reflection*). Copenhagen: Høst and Søn.

Wincentz Andersen, Jeanette. (2008). "Antropologiske aspekter i sager om æresrelateret drab" ("Anthropological Aspects on Honor-Related Murder"). In Arne Schmidt Møller (ed.), *Når æren er på spil—guidelines mod æresforbrydelser* (*When Honor Is at Stake—Guidelines against Honor Crimes*), 79–102. Århus: Forlaget SIESTA.

Newspapers

Berlingske Tidende, June 11, 2004.

Politiken, August 11, 2004.

Weekendavisen no. 35, August 23–29, 2004.

Berlingske Tidende, October 16, 2004.

Weekendavisen no. 18, April 30–May 1, 2008.

Notes

1. A contact person is a person who deals with authorities of any kind on behalf of a woman and helps her to learn how to cope in her new country.
2. In Norwegian: "De fleste av mine informanter er altså blitt gift arrangert, med mer eller mindre bruk av tvang."
3. The survey was conducted by the researchers Garbi Schmidt and Vibeke Jakobsen and was published in 2004.
4. See for example, *Berlingske Tidende*, June 11, 2004; *Politiken*, August 11, 2004; *Weekendavisen* no. 35, August 23–29, 2004.
5. IndSam, a former Danish umbrella organization for immigrants and refugees, was established in 1981.
6. Broen succeeded in having a crisis center for threatened women and minority adolescent girls established on August 1, 2005. On May 1, 2010, the crisis center was expanded to also receive couples who were fleeing forced marriage.

7. She contested the findings of Garbi Schmidt and Vibeke Jakobsen in a column in the daily paper *Berlingske Tidende* on October 16, 2004: 19.

8. Åsa Eldén and Jenny Westerstrand (2007: 39).

9. The ministry reluctantly accepted to postpone handling of applications for residence permits on the grounds of violence and thereby the expulsion of battered women until the committee's work was done.

10. In Storhaug (1998: 16), Muntaha, a participant in Storhaug's research, calls the traditional tea party a "meat market." See also Rushy Rashid (2000), who writes about the many tea parties where the parents of the young man come home to the woman's parents to ask for their daughter's hand in marriage.

11. Child marriages performed by imams seem to be on the rise, especially in the ghettos. The social consequences for the girls and political steps to stop the marriages are beyond the scope of this chapter.

12. Since the psychological implications and the harm the women suffer when they marry an unknown man are beyond the scope of this chapter, I refer to Ayaan Hirsi Ali (2005) and Hege Storhaug (2006).

13. In 2009 a Danish-Pakistani woman went with her two daughters to live for a period of time in Pakistan with her in-laws, while her Pakistani husband stayed in Denmark. She was shot dead by her husband's younger brother, presumably because she had an affair. As the Pakistani police did not provide the Danish police with any information, all charges against the husband were dropped. It has been alleged that liquidations are now committed in the men's country of origin out of fear of punishment (*Politiken*, July 1, 2008).

14. For instance, female genital mutilation (FGM) is called "circumcision" (*omskæring*), which thereby tones down the lifelong harm the custom is causing women (Banks et al. 2006). The Danish activist group Kvinder for Frihed (Women for Freedom) suggested a direct translation of FGM to Danish.

15. The most well-known being the liquidations of Sara and Fadime in Sweden (Wikan 2003; Eldén 2001), Anooshe in Norway (Storhaug 2006), and Sonay and Ghazala in Denmark (Schmidt Møller 2006; Kjær 2006).

16. A woman's family demands that she stay away from them, preferably at another location (city, country). If she disobeys, she risks being killed.

17. See for instance, Pnina Werbner (2007: 170).

18. The phrases "can cause a girl to lose her life," "a murder can happen," and "I actually feared death" are very odd ways to express that you

may be killed. I see the phrases as the women's detachment from the expressions.

19. Fadime was liquidated on January 21, 2002, and Ghazala on September 23, 2005.

20. Patrick died in a car accident in 1998. A police investigation established that his death was an accident, not a crime.

21. As for mothers or other female members' accomplice to murder, see Rose (2009), Güvercile (2003), Osmani (2000), Pervizat (2003), and Wikan (2003).

8

Language for Institutional Change

Notes from US Higher Education

Renate Klein, United States/United Kingdom

This chapter examines language and action for structural changes aimed at ending sexual assault and intimate partner violence on college campuses. The primary focus is on language used by campus authorities in reference to institutional operating procedures involved in staff development. This discussion draws on relevant policy and research but also on practical experience of working with, and learning from, staff members at universities across the United States who were active in violence prevention on campus.

The main proposition is that language for creating abuse-resistant institutional contexts must be language that is suited to guide practical changes to the institution's core operating procedures. Obviously, it is welcome when institutions issue statements in which they denounce abuse, which is preferable to witnessing the denial or dismissal of abuse. However, such statements too often are merely window dressing, which in itself does not promote structural change. What appears at least as important, and maybe more so in the long term, is mundane language that makes actions, such as building staff capacity for early intervention, core institutional responsibilities. Even though such operating procedures are not directly related to the teaching or research mission of universities, they underpin the proper functioning of the institutions. Procedures to ensure building safety, fire safety, proper heating and cooling, and the like are not optional but must be undertaken, even though they may rarely be associated with higher education proper.

Therefore language is needed that articulates abuse prevention as a core responsibility of an institution. Such language matters because the changes necessary to make institutions abuse resistant require sustained commitment through the ranks of institutional leadership. Antiviolence slogans articulate awareness of problems, which may be a precursor to making structural changes, but structural changes do not always, and certainly not automatically, follow from awareness.

In regard to institutions more generally as contexts for abuse, the spotlight of public debate in the United States has shone in particular on the Catholic Church,[1] the US armed forces,[2] and intermittently on college athletics departments, with the Penn State pedophilia scandal in 2012 a recent example.[3] The focus here is not on examining the language used in these debates but on language used in internal institutional procedures intended to address abuse.

Country Context

Research and legislation on the nexus of higher education, gender, and violence has a relatively long history in the United States and dates back to early equal opportunity legislation in which sexual assault was seen as an egregious form of sexual harassment (Title IX of the Education Amendments of 1972[4]). Title IX requires educational programs that receive federal financial assistance to prevent sexual harassment, including rape and sexual assault (recipients of federal financial assistance are public colleges and universities but also private schools if they receive some form of federal assistance such as student financial aid). Under Title IX, higher education institutions are required to investigate reports of sexual harassment and to take reasonable steps to end it and prevent its recurrence.

The first US surveys of rape on campus emerged in the 1980s and gave rise to systematic attempts to increase awareness and outreach, which continue to this day (Koss, Gidycz, and Wisniewski 1987). Among these have been awareness campaigns (such as Take Back the Night marches), so-called rape-prevention workshops for students, and the observation of dedicated awareness periods (so-called Awareness Months or Weeks) during which an issue is highlighted through lectures, movies, posters, flyers, panel discussions, and the like (Armstrong, Hamilton, and Sweeney

2006; Karjane, Fisher, and Cullen 2005). Outreach and awareness work has recently undergone a reframing as bystander intervention, in which students are taught to recognize and disrupt the buildup to a sexual assault (Banyard 2008; see also Klein 2012).

Evaluations of the effectiveness of rape-prevention workshops suggest that, if there are positive effects at all, they tend to be relatively short-lived changes in knowledge and attitudes (e.g., less victim blaming, higher accuracy of knowledge, less belief in rape myths). There is very little research evidence to suggest that such short educational sessions result in long-lasting behavior change (Anderson and Whiston 2005). However, the workshops may have other benefits, such as helping victims to connect with services or helping students to offer informal but better-informed support to friends who have been raped. Moreover, prevention programs are constantly evolving, and in particular those with proactive and interactive components (rather than lecturing to students) may be more effective in producing long-term behavioral change (Senn 2011; Rich 2010).[5]

Beginning in the 1990s, the Clery Act and Amendments required higher education institutions to publish campus crime statistics.[6] Although the systematic collection of crime statistics may help law enforcement and campus authorities to address crime, mere insistence on crime reporting is not necessarily effective for prevention (Sloan, Fisher, and Cullen 1997). Trying to force crime reporting does not address any of the reasons why people, in general, prefer not to report crime to authorities (although what happened might be told to a friend or other informal third party; Klein 2012). Campuses appear to be no exception; the vast majority of rapes and attempted rapes are not reported to campus authorities (Fisher, Daigle, Cullen, and Turner 2003). Reasons for not reporting to authorities include not thinking of an incident as a crime and lack of trust that authorities will be helpful. The latter includes fearing that authorities may not believe what is reported, blame the victim, fail to act on the report, or act in a way that does more harm than good. Campus authorities themselves may be ambivalent about getting crime reports, because passing these reports on to national crime-collection mechanisms or publishing them on university websites may harm the school's reputation.

Another important piece of legislation has been the Violence Against Women Act (VAWA) of 1994 and subsequent reauthorizations.[7] From 1999 on, this legislation included the appropriation of funds specifically for the higher education sector to strengthen campus responses to sexual assault, domestic and dating violence, and stalking.[8] Unlike Title IX and the Clery Act, VAWA was informed, especially in the beginning, by best practices developed in rape crisis centers and domestic violence projects. For instance, the campus grant program has required colleges and universities to create formal collaborative working relationships among offices and agencies in the manner of coordinated community responses, to provide or facilitate proper specialist victim support services, and to engage in institutional reform through the development of campus policies.[9]

From the 1980s to the present day, abuse on campus has been understood primarily as abuse among students, not among employees. Consequently, the bulk of awareness and outreach has focused on reaching students. Relatively few institutions seem to have addressed intimate abuses in a broader framework that also includes employees (the subsequent case study is an example).

Furthermore, by and large, relatively little antiviolence work has focused on institutional reform, compared to efforts invested in awareness campaigns. When there has been a focus on institutional reform, this has been concerned mostly with authoring student policies and less with other forms of institutional change, such as developing staff capacity to address abuse. As a result, the systematic integration into staff development of intervention and prevention skills is still at an early stage.

Finally, institutional responses may also be influenced by developments that tend to stay hidden from public view, but into which cases like the Penn State pedophilia scandal of 2012 occasionally afford a glimpse. Media reporting about this scandal has shed some light on the workings of "old boys" networks in higher education, in which influential individuals protect vested interests even if that contributes to abuse-conducive contexts (Zirin 2012).[10]

Within this context, US higher education responses to sexual assault and intimate partner violence on campus have been complex and contradictory. There is increasing recognition that abuse is an issue on campus, even though institutions may still be reluctant to say so in public because they are concerned with their reputation ("party school" appears to be an acceptable reputation; "rape school" is not). Awareness campaigns tend to be initiated and carried out by individual students or staff members, and their focus tends to be on highlighting the magnitude and impacts of abuse rather than on institutional change. That said, there certainly is recognition that abuse prevention also needs to include structural reforms.[11] Nonetheless, initiating such changes and maintaining any progress that has been made remains exceedingly difficult.

Academic Context

The focus here is exploring language used by campus authorities that may reveal how they frame the central problems in regard to abuse that the university, as an institution, ought to address. Such framings are not necessarily what institutional leadership may think about abuse in society in general. For instance, in the early 1990s a survey of US companies found that many human resources directors and company leaders said that the effects of domestic violence on employees were so severe that it affected the company's balance sheets (Roper Starch Worldwide for Liz Claiborne 1994). Despite this recognition, only about 12 percent of the same people said the company should do something about domestic violence, whereas about 88 percent felt intervention was the responsibility of local domestic violence projects. Employer attitudes have changed somewhat since then, but these responses demonstrate that organizations may be fully aware that abuse is a problem for the organization and yet maintain that somebody else ought to solve it. It is difficult to imagine that an organization would take a similar stance toward fire safety. If institutions are aware of the institutional impact of abuse, yet reluctant to consider systemic institutional reform, they appear to frame abuse, and intervention, as something unrelated to institutional processes and procedures, and thus unrelated to the institutional context.

To further analyze these framings, an informal third-party perspective is used to examine institutional context (Klein 2012), and policy-discourse analysis is used to examine institutional language (Allan 2003). Within this framework, two case examples of institutional language are discussed. One concerns language used to encourage crime reporting, which will be addressed under the heading "What We Must Know." The other example concerns decisions to develop staff capacity to intervene in abuse, which will be addressed under the heading "What We Must Do." The second example will be discussed in more detail, as it may illuminate the importance of mundane management language. As this discussion will show, "need to know" is a different policy framing than "need to do." Whereas "need to know" frames "not knowing" as the problem to be solved, which leaves the institutional operating procedures largely unchanged, "need to do" frames "not acting" at the problem to be solved, which sets the stage for making procedural changes.

Informal third parties—individuals in the social networks of victims and perpetrators—play an important role in supporting, and undermining, women's autonomy in their sexual and domestic relationships with men (Klein 2012). Among these network members are people at work such as coworkers, supervisors, and managers. Third parties, through their attitudes and behaviors toward both victims and perpetrators, shape access to victim support, influence the relative safety of public and private spaces, and influence responses to perpetrators. Informal third parties may not be legally responsible for crimes committed; this responsibility lies with the perpetrator(s). However, informal third parties contribute to contexts and local cultures that are more or less tolerant of sexual and domestic violence (Klein 2012). Abuse is not separate from but entangled with institutional structures and procedures (Hearn and Parkin 2001; Snyder, Scherer, and Fisher 2012). Indeed, the impacts of domestic violence in the workplace can be read as reflections of how workplaces deal with victims and perpetrators (Swanberg, Logan, and Macke 2006).

A central argument in policy discourse analysis is that social problems, as recognized problems, do not exist outside of discourses but instead are actively constructed through problem framings (Allan 2003). This reasoning is influenced by poststructuralist assumptions about the relationship between discourse and practice. These emphasize the active role of language, in particular language used by people in powerful positions, in shaping how we see reality and what appears to be a "given" social reality (Weedon 1997). Obviously, social life—the whole range of human activity in organizations, institutions, and societies—goes on regardless of framing, but what in the "ongoing, never-stand-still of the social" (Smith 2006: 2) is considered in need of a policy response is constructed through problem framings in policy discourses (illustrated, for instance, in the struggle of the Catholic Church to frame the apparently ongoing and hardly halting abuse of children by priests as a problem in need of a Church policy response).

This thinking implies that, if one was in a position to do so, one could pick and choose, so to speak, what to designate as a policy problem and what not. This, in turn, sets the stage for solutions in the form of policy responses to the problem as so designated. Policy discourse analysis aims to reveal this process by examining language used in policy documents. For the US higher education context, Elizabeth Allan (2003) found that university reports on the status of women constructed women's fear on campus as a problem within the wider issue of women's status. If the problem is decided to be women's fear (rather than pay gaps or the underrepresentation of women among full professors), measures to be taken to solve the problem would focus on reducing fear rather than equalizing pay or instituting policy to increase the number of women full professors (Allan 2003; for a similar analysis of university diversity reports, see Iverson 2008).

In this vein, to say then that rape and sexual assaults are problems on campus that need to be addressed is indicative of a problem framing in which the social reality of forced sex on campus (as documented in research and observations of rape crisis centers) is considered a campus problem in need of a campus response. This problem framing has been offered mostly by researchers and activists, and is shared by many campus practitioners including student services staff members and police officers.

In contrast, higher education institutions have had difficulty subscribing to this problem framing in full, which is evident in institutional language as illustrated subsequently but at first glance seems to contradict the relative readiness with which campuses talk about sexual assault. If anything, language denouncing sexual assault and intimate partner violence on campus is widespread, rape prevention work is relatively common, and since 1999 the federal campus grant-funding mechanism has enabled many campuses to develop or expand their awareness activities.

Yet the difficulty is in changing ingrained institutional practices. While institutions may use progressive language about sexual abuse, many responses address concerns that are derivative of the threat of rape rather than the threat of rape itself. Policy discourse analysis can be used to "read" these responses for the problem framings they reflect and to discern what about campus life has been designated as the sort of problem that needs a campus response. For instance, installing better outdoor lighting may address the so-designated problem of fear of walking on campus in darkness; cutting shrubs around buildings on campus responds to a so-designated problem of fear that somebody may jump out of the bushes and assault passersby; and installing emergency phones and distributing so-called rape whistles addresses the so-designated problem of how to sound alarm if needed. These policy responses have merits. Being able to sound alarm if needed is better than not being able to do so. It is a different matter, however, whether any of these measures contribute noticeably to a reduction in assaults, sexual assaults, stalking, or sexual harassment. These types of responses designate as problems a number of concerns from the perspective of potential victims. They do not designate as problems the behavior of perpetrators, nor do they designate as problems the concerns of actual victims who may want privacy and confidentiality, trustworthy and knowledgeable crisis support, and easy access to high-quality social, medical, and legal services.

"What We Must Know"

"Need to know" directives are one example of how campus authorities construct problems and subsequent policy responses. In these directives the campus community is encouraged, reminded, or admonished to report crime to campus authorities, and employees are encouraged to report crime to their supervisors. Receiving crime reports from students and employees enables campus authorities to compile crime statistics and publish these as required by law. "Need to know" directives thus frame as the problem the need of campuses to comply with legislation. While a legitimate concern, this is different from framing as the problem the recurrence of abuse or the lack of adequate victim support.

"Need to know" directives do not address the reasons most crime is not reported to authorities. In terms of underlying problem framing, such directives seem to assume that the reason people do not report is that they forget to do so or do not know where to report to. If these were the reasons people do not report crime, then reminders to do so, and where to do so, would be a solution. However, there is nothing in the empirical evidence that suggests these are the major reasons. As mentioned previously, reasons for not reporting domestic and sexualized abuse include people not being sure whether what they experienced or witnessed counts as a crime, and distrust of the authorities, which includes concern that reports may be dismissed and not taken seriously, that victims may be blamed, that no action will be taken, or that authorities will take action that is useless or does further harm (Fisher et al. 2003; Ullman 2010). Where authorities are not trusted, reminders to report to them seem futile. To overcome lack of trust, authorities need to build a track record of respectful and effective handling of cases of domestic and sexualized violence.

It is also a fallacy to think that campus authorities need yet another sexual assault to occur before they can take action. Action could be taken simply based on what has long been known about sexual assault and domestic violence, such as providing confidential disclosure opportunities and easy access to specialist victim services. Indeed, awareness and outreach activities, including campaigns, workshops, and bystander training, proceed effectively without knowledge of specific crimes committed. Waiting until crimes have been reported is akin to waiting for buildings to burn down before fire safety measures are put in place. Fire safety is a poor analogy to sexualized and domestic violence, but it is one of the things campuses seem to agree they must do, and not only after fire breaks out, but as a routine aspect of core operating procedure. With regard to fire safety, the institutional problem framing focuses squarely on preventative action.

"What We Must Do"

Detecting signs of abuse and facilitating access to proper victim services require considerable understanding and skill from higher education staff members. Developing these skills at a systemic, institutional level, rather than relying on individual staff to pick them up out of personal interest, is an organizational task that is different from hosting awareness campaigns. Developing staff capacity requires institutional resources. This may include hiring a victim-services provider to work directly on campus, setting up a systematic referral system with a community-based victim-services provider, or training staff on early intervention. In any case, these efforts need sustained staff development, which means specialized training, repeated every few years.

While staff members may be aware that rape and domestic violence are societal issues, a deeper understanding of impacts, dynamics, and risks is less common and often limited to those working for rape crisis centers and domestic violence projects. Through systematic staff development, university employees can develop deeper insight into the dynamics of sexual assault perpetration, coercive control in abusive relationships, the basics of victim support, and the advantages of coordinated action among campus and community partners (such as student health and counseling services, specialist victim services, law enforcement, campus housing, and academic advisers). Staff development, and supporting institutional policies and protocols, needs to enhance staff capacity to protect the confidentiality of a victim if the victim wishes to remain confidential (for instance, if a student does not want her parents to know that she was raped. Parents may or may not be supportive of their daughter; if she asks university staff members for confidentiality, staff members should respect this; Karjane, Fisher, and Cullen 2005). Staff members also need to be able to maintain a nonjudgmental attitude (and may have to struggle with their own prejudices and stereotypes in the process), support a victim's decision making (rather than assuming they know best what the victim should do), and make proper referrals to further resources (which requires detailed knowledge of which services are in reach and which are not). All this is easier said than done. The praxis experience, by and large, has shown that these skills do not necessarily come easy, and their development requires a certain amount of dedicated training and practice.

Capacity development can be done by sending staff members to conferences or workshops, or it can be done in house. The latter may be more cost effective, because specialist victim-services providers (who often charge modest rates) can be brought in from the local community or region and address a large number of staff members at once.

Thus the financial costs to the institution are likely to be relatively small. However, in-house training does mean that staff will need time off, even if it is only for a few hours. It may also mean that staff members need to be motivated, encouraged, or directed to attend training. This, in turn, means that immediate supervisors and managers must be supportive of training, which may mean that the supervisors further up in the institutional hierarchy may need to be on board as well. Thus making these sorts of changes to an institution's operating procedures requires considerable leadership support at multiple levels of the organizational hierarchy.

Institutions often use written policy documents to establish the institution's stance on sexual assault or domestic violence and to provide guidance for students and staff on what to do when problems arise. For the individuals who write, vet, and formally adopt such policies, the policy development process in itself may be a useful awareness-raising and learning experience. However, merely having such a policy on the books is not enough; it is also necessary to develop staff capacity to put the policy into action. The social and interpersonal dynamics of sexual assault and domestic violence are too complex to leave them up to well-intentioned language in policy documents, which few people will be aware of unless the documents are used to actually develop staff capacity.

Awareness campaigns may be a necessary first step toward institutional change, but they are probably not sufficient. At some point, institutional leadership must pick up the torch and initiate the transformation of institutional operating procedures. This kind of initiative is likely to be verbalized, and if it is verbalized in public, one can see what sort of language is used for the purpose of initiating changes in operating procedures and how that language compares with other institutional language about abuse.

Case Study and Discussion

In 2006, the university where I worked authored and implemented an employee policy on the impact of domestic violence in the workplace. All employees—clerical support staff, professionals, and research and teaching staff—were to receive a two-hour orientation on how domestic violence affects the workplace and on the purpose of the policy. There were numerous training sessions, delivered by a three-person team, which included a campus-based victim-services provider, an employee from the university's human resources department, and a staff member of the local domestic violence project. Employees could also volunteer to become a "responder"—somebody in the workplace who could serve as an informal support person and a link to further resources. Responders received a three-hour training that included more practical exercises on how to respond to disclosures of abuse, make referrals, or open a conversation about abuse. Many employees were enthusiastic about the new policy and attended training. Within a year more than one hundred responders were listed on the university's website, and approximately one third of all employees had been trained.

At the time, I worked closely with the group who developed the policy, which afforded some insight into the organizational effort it may take to get employees to attend policy training. High employee turnout was an important goal. Training a critical mass of employees should increase staff capacity to address issues appropriately and would constitute a transformation toward early intervention and prevention. The university did not have systematic staff development on this topic, and the operational procedure for dealing with domestic violence was to address individual cases only when they had reached crisis proportion.

Thus attendance and turnout mattered. While turnout may reflect individual interest, framing staff development on this matter in terms of individual interest seemed insufficient. Instead, the impact of domestic violence on the workplace is a matter of collective interest. Thus institutional leadership needed to take the steps necessary to make it clear that abuse prevention is in the interest of all employees, not only those personally affected.

Because academic staff were initially slow to sign up to the training initiative, my colleague and I met with the deans of the six larger academic and professional divisions to discuss how to shift the momentum from lackluster attendance to more engaged participation. We explained the purpose of the new policy (each division had indeed had to deal with cases of domestic violence) and asked the deans to encourage their staff members to attend one of the training sessions offered. Although teaching and research staff formally report to deans (either directly or through directors), deans usually do not order academic employees around (at least not at this university). However, deans can encourage and set examples, and, if they choose to do so, they can frame participation as a matter of collective responsibility rather than personal interest.

The deans were responsive to our request and their overall approach was similar in that they sent electronic memos to faculty encouraging participation in training. However, the details of their approaches differed. These differences included the wording used in the memos, the actions of the deans and whether they themselves attended training and thus role-modeled attendance, and the organizational structure of the six divisions along with the extent to which they were used to complying with training requests.

Turnout differed noticeably among the six divisions. Three of the deans' appeals were considered "strong," resulting in significant turnout of up to 40 percent of employees. Strong appeals included language that explicitly stated the dean's support of the training ("in support of this initiative I . . ."; "I am so committed to this effort that . . ."), language in which deans emphasized their expectation that all employees attend ("I want all employees to attend . . ."; "I want every member [of the division] to attend . . ."; "I am expecting 100% attendance from the [unit] at an orientation session"), and language for articulating collective responsibility ("I have dedicated the first [unit meeting] to the [policy training] so that we can attend a professional development session with our colleagues"; "[the unit] will sponsor several orientation sessions. All [unit] employees are asked to attend one of these professional development sessions with our colleagues"; "I have learned that [unit members] have attended a session, and they are very enthusiastic about their value").

At least two of the deans with strong appeals attended one of the training sessions themselves. These two divisions also had supportive features related to organizational structure and organizational culture. One had an ethos of supporting social justice issues, and the division with the highest turnout was, as a recipient of major federal funding streams, used to compliance with training requirements (as may be attached to grant funding); the most visible sign of this structure was the position of a compliance officer, who also was extremely helpful in fielding employee questions about the new policy and directing them to training sessions.

From the division with the lowest turnout, no dean's language was available, and it is unclear if and how this dean framed an appeal to the division's employees. In another "weak" appeal (in terms of relatively low turnout), the language used was vague about the dean's support of the initiative ("employees need to understand [the new policy] . . ."; "[other units] have been invited to attend these and similar workshops already, and the remaining Colleges will soon follow suit . . ."). The weak appeal was tentative in terms of what the dean expected from the employees ("So I encourage you to attend . . .") and did not make a case for collective responsibility.

After the training sessions had been completed, I had the opportunity to ask some of the deans with strong appeals why they had supported the policy training. As one might expect, they said that domestic violence was an important problem. However, the dean of the division with the highest turnout, who at the time was relatively new to the university, also said, "I thought this is something else we had to do." This is perhaps not a rousing antiviolence slogan, but it is instead clear and unequivocal language about institutional responsibility. For this dean, addressing domestic violence was as firmly on the agenda as the other problems he had to address—"something we needed to do, not something extra."

Conclusion

The main proposition was that language for creating abuse-resistant contexts must be language that is suited to guide practical changes in an institution's core operating procedures. This was elaborated in terms of language used in university contexts by campus authorities. An informal third-party perspective and policy-discourse analysis provided a theoretical rationale. Drawing on practical experience in higher education in the United States, examples of leadership language were examined to illuminate what appears to be a key challenge in creating abuse-resistant working and learning environments: the transformation of institutional operating procedures. In this transformation, institutional leadership has an important role. College campuses in the United States have a long history of responding to sexual and domestic violence. Many campus authorities may be well intentioned, but the language used in policy statements often suggests that authorities misunderstand, or do not take seriously, the social, cultural, and interpersonal dynamics of abuse. The case example shed light on how language, leadership, and organizational responses to abuse prevention may be entwined. For the practical business of transforming basic operating procedures so that organizations and workplaces become safer environments, plain language about assuming institutional responsibility may be as important, if not more, than rhetorical flourishes about rape culture or the scourge of domestic violence.

References

Allan, Elizabeth J. (2003). "Constructing Women's Status: Policy Discourses of University Women's Commissions." *Harvard Educational Review* 73 (1): 44–72.

Anderson, L. A., and S. C. Whiston. (2005). "Sexual Assault Education Programs: A Meta-Analytic Examination of Their Effectiveness." *Psychology of Women Quarterly* 29: 374–88.

Armstrong, E. A., L. Hamilton, and B. Sweeney. (2006). "Sexual Assault on Campus: A Multilevel, Integrative Approach to Party Rape." *Social Problems* 53 (4): 483–99.

Banyard, V. L. (2008). "Sexual Violence: Current Perspectives on Prevention and Intervention." *Journal of Prevention & Intervention in the Community* 36 (1–2): 1–4.

Fisher, B. S., L. E. Daigle, F. T. Cullen, and M. G. Turner. (2003). "Reporting Sexual Victimization to the Police and Others: Results from a National-Level Study of College Women." *Criminal Justice and Behavior* 30: 6–38.

Hearn, J., and W. Parkin. (2001). *Gender, Sexuality and Violence in Organizations: The Unspoken Forces of Organization Violations.* London: Sage.

Iverson, S. V. (2008). "Now Is the Time for Change: Reframing Diversity Planning at Land-Grant Universities." *Journal of Extension* [Online] 46 (1): Article IFEA3, http://www.joe.org/joe/2008/february/a3.shtml.

Karjane, H. M., B. S. Fisher, and F. T. Cullen. (2005). *Sexual Assault on Campus: What Colleges and Universities Are Doing about It*. Washington, DC: Office of Justice Programs, US Department of Justice.

Klein, R. (2012). *Responding to Sexual and Domestic Violence against Women: The Role of Informal Networks*. New York: Cambridge University Press.

Koss, M. P., C. A. Gidycz, and N. Wisniewski. (1987). "The Scope of Rape: Incidence and Prevalence of Sexual Aggression and Victimization in a National Sample of Higher Education Students." *Journal of Counseling and Clinical Psychology* 55 (2): 162–70.

Rich, M. D. (2010). "The interACT Model: Considering Rape Prevention from a Performance Activism and Social Justice Perspective." *Feminism & Psychology* 20 (4): 511–28.

Roper Starch Worldwide for Liz Claiborne. (1994). *Addressing Domestic Violence: A Corporate Response*. New York: Roper Starch.

Senn, C. Y. (2011). "An Imperfect Feminist Journey: Reflections on the Process to Develop an Effective Sexual Assault Resistance Programme for University Women." *Feminism &Psychology* 21 (1): 121–37.

Sloan, J. J., B. S. Fisher, and F. T. Cullen. (1997). "Assessing the Student-Right-to-Know and Campus Security Act of 1990: An Analysis of the Victim Reporting Practices of College and University Students." *Crime & Delinquency* 43: 48–168.

Smith, Dorothy E. (2006). *Institutional Ethnography as Practice*. Lanham: Rowman and Littlefield.

Snyder, J. A., H. L. Scherer, and B. S. Fisher. (2012). "Social Organization and Social Ties: Their Effects on Sexual Harassment Victimization in the Workplace." *Work: Journal of Prevention, Assessment & Rehabilitation* 42 (1): 137–50.

Swanberg, J. E., T. K. Logan, and C. Macke. (2006). "The Consequences of Partner Violence on Employment and the Workplace." In E. K. Kelloway, J. Barling, and J. J. Hurrell (eds.), *Handbook of Workplace Violence*, 351–79. Thousand Oaks, CA: Sage.

Ullman, S. E. (2010). *Talking about Sexual Assault: Society's Response to Survivors*. Washington, DC: American Psychological Association.

Weedon, Chris. (1997). *Feminist Practice and Postructuralist Theory*. Oxford: Blackwell.

Zirin, Dave. (2012). "Why the NCAA's Sanctions on Penn State Are Just Dead Wrong." *Edge of Sports*. Accessed August 14, 2012, http://www.edgeofsports.com/2012-07-23-761/index.html.

Notes

1. http://www.boston.com/globe/spotlight/abuse (Accessed 8/21/2012).
2. http://usnews.nbcnews.com/_news/2012/01/18/10184222-panetta-could-be-19000-military-sex-assaults-each-year?lite (Accessed 8/21/2012).
3. http://www.cbsnews.com/2718-400_162-1332.html?tag=storyMediaBox;postSpecialReport (Accessed 8/21/2012).
4. http://www.dol.gov/oasam/regs/statutes/titleix.htm (Accessed 8/21/2012).
5. http://www.cmhc.utexas.edu/vav_peertheatre.html (Accessed 8/21/2012).
6. http://www.securityoncampus.org/summary-jeanne-clery-act (Accessed 8/21/2012).
7. http://www.ovw.usdoj.gov/legislation.htm (Accessed 8/21/2012).
8. http://www.ovw.usdoj.gov/ovwgrantprograms.htm#1 (Accessed 8/21/2012).
9. http://www.ovw.usdoj.gov/overview.htm (Accessed 8/21/2012).
10. http://chronicle.com/article/Penn-States-Culture-of/132853 (Accessed 8/21/2012).
11. http://www.preventioninstitute.org/index.php?option=com_jlibrary&view=article&id=105&Itemid=127 (Accessed 8/21/2012).

Notes on Contributors

Stéphanie Condon is a demographer and social geographer at the Institut national d'études démographiques (National Institute of Demography) in Paris, France.

Daniela Gloor is a sociologist at Social Insight, an independent research institute in Switzerland.

Jeff Hearn is a British sociologist and professor at Hanken School of Economics, Finland.

Renate Klein is a psychologist and professor at London Metropolitan University, England, and is affiliated with the University of Maine.

Anna Kwiatkowska is a psychologist and professor at the Polish Academy of Sciences.

Hanna Meier is a sociologist at Social Insight, an independent research institute in Switzerland.

Britta Mogensen is a Danish anthropologist and activist.

Bo Wagner Sørensen is an anthropologist at Roskilde University, Denmark.

Carole Wright is a sociologist at University of Huddersfield, England.

Index

Printed and bound in the United States of America

DATE DUE	RETURNED
MAR 3 0 2016	APR 1 1 2016

MAR 3 0 2015   APR 1 4 2016

0 1341 1464419 5